Beyond Your Wildest Dreams

Prepare yourself for the greatest magickal adventure you have ever experienced. Touch a soul-gratifying source of unconditional love and fill your life with positive energy for spiritual growth. Reach new heights of enlightenment and ecstasy beyond your wildest dreams through the magick of *Astral Love*. Let this no-nonsense guide to the once secret practices of astral travel and sex magick take you on the most exciting mystical journey of your life.

Open new avenues of magickal practice with astral lovers who will teach you the ecstasy of higher-plane intimacy. If you are single and without a reliable partner, astral sex can be a safe and rewarding alternative to a physical relationship. Your astral partner can even help find the right person for you, when you are ready. Develop strong spiritual ties with advanced beings who will become your teachers, friends and lovers through the practice of astral sex magick.

Whatever your personal path or practices, *Astral Love* provides you with everything you will need to explore the astral realm safely and with confidence. Learn how to access this incredibly powerful force for self exploration and renewal through a variety of rituals and meditations. Discover your true nature through a full set of in-depth self examinations based upon each of the light-centers of your body. Enjoy the warm embrace and lingering glow of an astral lover who will enrich your life and satisfy your emotional needs. Experience the ultimate thrill of *Astral Love*.

About the Author

I have always been close to Nature. As a child, I spent a great amount of time outdoors by myself. Trees, herbs, and flowers become part of my indoor and outdoor landscapes wherever I live. My reading covers vast areas of history, the magickal arts, philosophy, customs, mythology, and fantasy. I have studied every part of the New Age religions from Eastern philosophy to Wicca. I hope I never stop learning and expanding.

I live a rather quiet life in the company of my husband and my four cats, with occasional visits with my children and grandchildren. I collect statues of dragons and wizards, crystals and other stones, and of course, books. Most of my time is spent researching and writing. Before I am finished with one book, I am working on another in my head. All in all, I am just an ordinary Pagan person.

To Write to the Author

If you wish to contact the author or would like more information about this book, please write to the author in care of Llewellyn Worldwide, and we will forward your request. Both the author and publisher appreciate hearing from you and learning of your enjoyment of this book. Llewellyn Worldwide cannot guarantee that every letter written to the author will be answered, but all will be forwarded. Please write to:

D. J. Conway
℅ Llewellyn Worldwide
P.O. Box 64383-K161, St. Paul, MN 55164-0383, U.S.A.

Please enclose a self-addressed stamped envelope for reply, or $1.00 to cover costs. If outside U.S.A., enclose international postal reply coupon.

Free Catalog from Llewellyn Worldwide

For more than 90 years, Llewellyn has brought its readers knowledge in the fields of metaphysics and human potential. Learn about the newest books in spiritual guidance, natural healing, astrology, occult philosophy, and more. Enjoy book reviews, new age articles, a calendar of events, plus current advertised products and services. To get your free copy of *Llewellyn's New Worlds of Mind and Spirit*, send your name and address to:

Llewellyn's New Worlds of Mind and Spirit
P.O. Box 64383-K161, St. Paul, MN 55164-0383, U.S.A.

Llewellyn's Tantra & Sexual Arts Series

Astral Love

Romance, Ecstasy & Higher Consciousness

D. J. Conway

1996
Llewellyn Publications
St. Paul, MN 55164-0383, U.S.A.

FIRST EDITION
First Printing, 1996

Cover painting: Dorian Dyer
Book design, layout, and editing: Designed To Sell

Library of Congress Cataloging-in-Publication Data
Conway, D.J. (Deanna J.)
      Astral love: romance, ecstasy & higher consciousness
/ D.J. Conway. -- 1st ed.
        p. cm. -- (Llewellyn's tantra & sexual arts series)
      Includes bibliographical references.
      ISBN 1-56718-161-9 (trade pbk.)
      1. Astral projection. 2. Love--Miscellanea 3. Magic.
      I. Title.   II. Series.
BF1389.A7C623   1995
133.903-95; sh38 11-21-95--dc20   95-42624
                                                 CIP

Printed in the United States of America

Llewellyn Publications
A Division of Llewellyn Worldwide, Ltd.
P.O. Box 64383, St. Paul, MN 55164-0383

About Llewellyn's Tantra & Sexual Arts Series

There is perhaps no other kind of magical power more widely available to each and every human being as the magical power inherent in human sexual energies. Yet these energies have historically been suppressed and made taboo to such an extent that they have become energies that often seem to be of the most "forbidden" kind.

Llewellyn's Tantra and Sexual Arts Series represents a bold attempt to get beyond these often unnecessary limitations and restrictions and to explore the field of the spiritual and magical uses of human sexual energies in a free and enlightened manner. This is our spiritual birthright as human beings.

In the series, our authors will delve into practical applications of both Eastern and Western forms of sexual spirituality, such as Tantrism and sexual magick. But there will also be works which explore the ideas and practices of sexual arts not directly linked to specific magical or spiritual traditions but which nevertheless have a spiritual quality. The practice of sexual arts in our modern world is an element of life which holds its own fascination and deserves attention in its own right. The concepts contained in Llewellyn's Tantra and Sexual Arts Series will act as gateways into this wondrous and sometimes mysterious world.

Our modern society is fascinated by—and often enslaved to—sexual energies. The works of this series will help readers and students make use of these energies to help and heal the body, mind, and heart and to liberate the whole topic of human sexuality so that it can at last reach its full potential in our modern world.

Other Books by the Author

Celtic Magic
Norse Magic
The Ancient & Shining Ones
Maiden, Mother, Crone
Dancing With Dragons
By Oak, Ash & Thorn
Flying Without a Broom
Moon Magick
Animal Magick
Falcon Feather & Valkyrie Sword

Fiction

The Dream Warrior

Forthcoming

Magickal, Mythical, Mystical Beasts
Soothslayer (fiction)
Lord of Shadow & Light

Contents

Introduction

When I was first approached about writing this book, I was very hesitant. After all, just being a Pagan is often enough for some people to think you are half a brick shy of a load, without divulging what you know about physical sex magick, and astral love and sex magick in the bargain.

For centuries, physical sex magick has been used, and sometimes misused, by magicians. Its esoteric use is still found in the Great Rite of Wicca, Tantra, and certain rituals of ceremonial magick. Unfortunately, it is also an excuse to misuse women (and sometimes men) in certain so-called Pagan groups.

Knowledge of sex magick can be misused and abused by those who understand little, if any, of the esoteric wisdom behind it. These types of people never listen when you caution them that misuse will bring disastrous results. Even if this knowledge were not available in books, these people would sooner or later discover about sex magick in its many forms anyway. This is because these types of people search for reasons to have physical sex with a wide variety of partners in ways which they feel excuse them for unethical behavior and lack of responsibility.

This book is NOT about physical sex magick. It is not even about sex as understood in the usual terms. It is about astral love and astral sex magick, which are totally different. There is a bibliography at the end of this book listing sources which refer to physical sex magick. If you choose to involve yourself in these activities, be certain you are not coercing or influencing anyone to join you against their will. Be very certain you are performing sex magick for the appropriate reasons, not for the thrills.

If you plan to go into astral love and sex magick for the thrills, forget it. It's easier to join a rowdy singles' group or the local mate-swapping party. This physical activity brings much quicker gratification than astral love, and at a fraction of the effort and time. Astral love and sex magick are advanced magickal techniques; an ancient knowledge once reserved for selected people who had passed through rigorous initiations. In this age of drug-resistant diseases which can kill you, members of the opposite (or same) sex who stalk and prey after one date, con artists who are only after your money and property, I feel it is time to release this information to the Pagan community at large.

Self-responsibility and self-knowledge are the key words to positive, successful love and sex magick in the astral, but you will have no one to look over your shoulder to chastise you if you are doing it for the wrong reasons. Be certain of why you want to love an astral being, why you want to learn this type of magick, and why you want to use it before you ever get involved. Each magician, whatever magick she or he performs, is responsible for her or his reasoning behind the use of that magick, and no one else. No one can "buy you out" if the magick backfires, because you are unethical in your actions and motives.

Properly done, this type of magick is one of the most powerful there is. It can enhance your life, filling it with love, compassion, understanding, and positive energy in all ways and on all levels. If you persevere, you can raise your spiritual level to new heights, beyond anything you thought possible.

The ultimate goal of any true magick should be spiritual enlightenment and growth. If you set your sights on this, it is unlikely you will go astray.

One

❧

The Astral Plane

To even begin to understand about astral love, you must first know about the astral plane itself and its inhabitants. Then you must practice getting out onto this astral plane. This may sound simple enough, but there are rules and precautions which it is wise to observe, just as you would not wander about in a large city or strange country without some preparation to make certain you got to the correct destination and stayed out of dangerous areas.

Modern-day humans are divided in their opinions about the existence of the astral plane and the ability of individuals to go there or to communicate with its inhabitants. Disbelief runs into difficulty when people inadvertently experience the astral plane for themselves. In this day of scientists and their so-called "reality," it has become fashionable to laugh at the existence of the astral plane. This attitude results in people who experience the astral plane "by chance," not talking about what has occurred. However, in a poll taken by the Llewellyn *New Worlds of Mind & Spirit* magazine in 1993,

1

sixty-three percent of the people answering the poll said that they successfully astral traveled on a regular basis.

Cultures around the world have known of the existence of the astral plane since the earliest attempts of humankind to contact the gods, guiding spirits, and deceased relatives. The name for the astral plane may differ from culture to culture, but the basic description of it and what it contains are the same. The predominant, male-god-only religions of the Christians, Moslems, and Hebrews have strict taboos against believing in or contacting this plane of existence. (If it doesn't exist, why the taboos against it?) When members of these religions experience the astral plane, the religious leaders immediately classify the experience as imaginary, the work of demons, or an angelic communication from god. Worse yet, if you should find an astral lover, the orthodox religions will classify you as mentally unbalanced, or more likely, possessed by devils. This is a strange reaction from religions which on the one hand say this experience is impossible, since spirits can't have satisfying "physical" contact with the living, yet on the other hand go into a panic about such "sinful" experiences with "demons." At the same time, Christians talk about Mary's conception by a "spirit" as an extremely holy occurrence.

Shamans the world over have always known about astral travel, using it as a vital part of their rituals. Shamanism goes beyond Native Americans, Eskimos, and the Lapps; at one time the religious practice of shamanism was known throughout the Mediterranean and Europe. Stories tell of the shaman, or religious psychic, reaching the flying state by climbing a ladder, tree, or tent pole, and turning into a bird, riding off on a flying horse, or experiencing some similar method of travel. Even the later Christian "saints" wrote of seven steps leading to heaven. The religious leaders of certain non-Aryan people of India still enter their astral trances by riding a horse-headed stick, as did the Sufis of the Middle Ages.

Records in history and mythology tell of examples of astral travel as far back as ancient Egypt, Greece, and Mesopotamia, if not earlier. It was known in India, and in the Celtic and Norse cultures, as well as being an ability credited to yogins and alchemists. History and mythology are full of veiled references to astral travel, proving it is nothing new to humans. It was once considered a vital and necessary part of spiritual development for initiates, and is a natural part of your psychic make-up, whether you like it or not. You do it every night during sleep, even though you may not remember your experience.

The astral plane occupies the same space as the physical world, is separate from it, yet interpenetrates it. Everything that exists in this universe vibrates at various speeds and cycles. The higher the vibration, the less dense the object. The astral plane and its inhabitants vibrate at an extremely high rate, making them invisible to the physical eye. We are constantly surrounded by the astral plane and those who live there, but we are ordinarily unaware of it. The method of reaching the astral, therefore, cannot be by physical means.

All traditions which believe in the astral plane say it contains multiple levels, with higher and lower areas for deceased humans and other entities. The most common number of levels mentioned is seven, which may be related to the seven major chakras of the astral body. Each level gently merges with the one above it except for the very highest plane, which is actually above the seven levels, and not numbered among them. It is impossible to enter this highest of astral levels, for the vibrations are too refined. Only the Supreme Creative Power (the Creator-Creatrix behind the Gods) and a very few attendants/messengers exist there. The seventh level, directly below this, is the plane of the deity archetypes, those powerful entities we know as the Gods. The beings of this level can bring you up to them, or they can come down to you. Only spiritual (not religious) preparation can gain you entrance to this area.

The five intermediate levels range from areas for those who are just beginning to be aware of spiritual responsibility to sections for those who have advanced in their studies over several lifetimes. These are the astral levels you want to actively seek in your travels. In these areas you can expect to be protected and guided to the teacher or being who will help you. Nature spirits, beings which we now call mythical, and the souls of animals also dwell within these middle levels. So do strongly created human thoughtforms.

At the other end of this series of astral planes is the lowest level, an area of spiritual darkness inhabited by malevolent thoughtforms, earthbound spirits, and devolved human souls. Sometimes you find souls there who think they must suffer in hell; however, when these deceased humans decide the punishment is no longer necessary, they are allowed to rise to a suitable higher level. The ancient practice of praying for the dead has a mystical reason behind it because, if they chose to do so, the dead can be aware of the living. Prayers said for them can convince them to give up their self-created hell and move to more comfortable surroundings. The thoughtform of the orthodox "devil" is confined to this lowest of levels, but you have to believe in this entity for it to have power over you.

The terms "higher" and "lower" have no relationship with social classes, religion, outward personal appearance while on Earth, or how much time a person spent in spiritual pursuits. A spirit earns its place on a level by the manner in which it lived its earthly life, and the way it sought (or didn't seek) spiritual growth. This is the real meaning of karma. (Please understand that the word "spiritual" has absolutely nothing to do with religious denominations or churches.)

There are no definite road maps for travel on the astral planes. Each of us must discover our way through these Otherworld levels, although the descriptions given by other astral travelers can assist us. By observation, we learn to take note of markers which help us return to or avoid an area.

Traveling to the Astral

If one doesn't get onto the astral through the physical body, what does one use to get there? Ancient writers were quite specific about humans having more than one body. The Upanishads of India speak of two invisible bodies, plus the gross physical one. Some beliefs list as many as seven to nine different bodies, or as few as three. The ancient Egyptian descriptions of these subtle bodies seem to correspond to the seven light centers, or chakras of the Eastern beliefs. In some manner they may also relate to the seven astral levels. Unfortunately, we no longer have any information to help us understand the connection.

The physical body, however, is well understood. It is the form with which you are most familiar—what you probably call "you." The mental body is a collection of the mental vibrations which make up you as the interior, thinking person. The emotional body is built from the emotional state of your being, positive or negative. This body changes the most, because your emotions change often. It projects its state of true being directly into the aura (the envelope of energy surrounding the physical body and seen by psychics), sometimes causing flares of color.

Some people call the astral body the emotional body, probably because the emotions tend to accompany a person while astral traveling. To me, this astral form appears more to be what is known in various cultures as the "double." When you travel through the astral worlds, either deliberately or while asleep, you travel in this body. It is a duplicate of the physical body, but in a nebulous form, with the ability to move freely wherever it wants, through time and space. Finally, the spiritual body may well be called the soul. It is the most etheric of the subtle bodies, and does not leave the vicinity of the physical body until death. For simplicity, in this book I will be concerned only with the physical and astral bodies.

Under special circumstances, the energy of the astral body can actually be photographed using Kirlian photography. This method was discovered by a Russian scientist, Semyon Kirlian, in the early 1940s, when he was studying what he called bioplasma. Later, in France, scientists began to weigh dying people, and discovered a discrepancy after death of a few ounces for which they could not account. Dr. Duncan McDougall in England and Dr. Zaalberg Van Zelst in The Hague, working independently, both arrived at the same displaced amount: 69.5 grams. Then they decided to take photos using infrared rays. These pictures showed a luminous cloud, in the exact shape of the body, exiting at the time of death. This form is the astral body accompanied by the soul.

Astral travel is accomplished when the astral body temporarily leaves the physical body and moves out onto the astral plane. The astral and physical bodies are constantly connected by what some people call the "silver cord." Such travel is no more dangerous or difficult than driving a car, as long as you obey the rules, use common sense, and show concern for yourself and others. Some writers insist that you are not really astral traveling unless you can look back and see your physical body. This isn't necessarily true. Dreams of falling, flying, or gliding are memories of astral travel during sleep. Waking to the sound of someone (not there) calling your name falls into this category, as does being in deep meditation or contemplation during which you are totally unaware of your physical body.

When you are out in the astral, you may or may not see the silver cord. There are many opinions on where this cord is attached: Some people see it attached to their ankle; others see it coming from their solar plexus. If I am aware of this cord at all, I see it attached to the center of my forehead in the area of the brow chakra. I don't feel there is one right answer to this question of attachment. Just know the cord exists and is at all times your connection with your physical body. Also know that, contrary to reports, this cord cannot be cut accidentally, leaving you somewhere in limbo. There are all kinds of horror stories about evil entities attacking and severing the silver cord. The negative beings I have met were never interested in my cord, but in me. If you surround yourself with the white light before going to sleep or astral traveling, you will be in no danger from such entities, even though encounters with them may make you uncomfortable.

Astral projection and travel are influenced by the mind— that mysterious "something" often considered to be part of the brain. The brain and the mind, however, are different things. The brain is a physical organ of the body, while the mind is very elusive—the part of you that feels, perceives, thinks, remembers, and wills. Science has no idea where the mind is located nor any explanation of its functions. We do know that, physically, the brain is divided into two hemispheres: the left and right brains. Although these divisions are connected by a mass of tissue called the Corpus Callosum, their functions are distinctly different.

The right brain is associated with the subconscious mind, which deals with creativity and imagination; the left brain is analytical and linear. The two hemispheres are con-

nected, enabling communication between them. Use of the
subconscious mind is evidenced by Alpha brainwaves of
eight to thirteen cycles per second, as compared to the conscious mind's Beta waves of fourteen to eighteen or more
cycles per second. The subconscious mind has ten times the
power of the conscious mind. Reaching the subconscious
mind is the preparatory stage of astral travel.

The third part of the mind is the superconscious, so
named by Carl Jung. When you sink into this area, your brainwaves drop into the Theta rhythm of four to seven cycles per
second and you are in deep meditation, trance, or are astral
traveling. Full communication with astral entities, deities, or
teachers can only be accomplished while in this state.

Only ten percent of your mind's potential is accessible
while using the conscious mind and its Beta waves. To tap the
other ninety percent one must go deeper into the Alpha-
Theta areas. This is called an "altered state of consciousness,"
where, once we accept what we are "seeing," our physical
nervous system begins to experience it.

Some people should never engage in deliberate astral
travel. Psychiatrists, metaphysicians, and bio-feedback pro-
fessionals all agree that depressive neurotics, epileptics, the
mentally ill, drug users (of any kind, except prescription
drugs which don't cloud the mind in any way), and those
highly susceptible to the will of others, all should avoid
deliberately going into the Alpha-Theta states, because the
experience could make their conditions worse. I would also
advise those with bad heart trouble against entering this
state, which alters heart rate and respiration, and could be
dangerous to people suffering from serious heart disease.
Finally, to this list, I would add those who are unwilling to
face the truth of their actions and life.

You don't need to work in a group situation to learn how
to astral travel or to enter an altered state of consciousness,

and too many of these groups are only interested in getting your money and possibly control of your life. You don't need an expensive mind-training course. If you are sincere in your efforts and have no serious physical or mental problems, you can learn to get there on your own, and save your money for more productive things. You can proceed at your own pace, free of someone else's spiritual beliefs, and know exactly who is in control: YOU.

It is unnecessary and very dangerous to use drugs to help you separate the astral body from the physical body. You want your mind to be totally under *your* control during astral travel; with drugs you have little or no control. Getting into the astral while under the influence of alcohol or drugs is almost certain to project you straight onto the lowest astral levels, where all the negative entities hang out. Besides, it is a scientific fact that the brain produces its own chemical "high." In 1959, research at Yale University revealed that the pineal gland (connected with the brow chakra) secretes melatonin—a derivative of serotonin—which is similar in molecular structure to LSD. Other studies in neurochemistry found that the brain also produces other natural consciousness-altering drugs, such as dimethyltryptamine, during deep, relaxed meditation. These natural drugs appear to have a direct bearing on the intensity of astral travel and what you experience while on the astral planes. The more you practice meditation and astral travel, the quicker you reach this natural high and the stronger it is.

The astral body has fewer limitations in what it can do than the physical body. For instance, you can move from one place to another instantly, simply by thinking of doing so. Paracelsus, in *Selected Writings*, said that the astral body can go through walls without harm or destruction, can move forward and backward through time, and enter what is commonly known among shamans as the Otherworlds. What would be a barrier to the physical body is nothing to the astral body. Even if a very psychic person in the physical should see you, he or she can't detain you or hamper you in any way.*

Don't worry about all the negative propaganda created to frighten you away from astral travel. You will not lose your soul, get stuck and be unable to return, or die. These are all myths, created to discourage anyone from discovering that orthodox religions might not have all the answers to spiritual issues. The same applies to teachers who tell you that something bad will happen unless you meditate only with them. All this does is ensure those teachers of a constant group of followers to control.

You may encounter many methods of achieving astral travel. Some books talk about "willing" yourself out of your physical body; but when beginners try this method and fail, they often assume they lack ability, or that the whole thing is just so much marsh gas. Some books describe a method of removing your astral body from your physical body by visualizing yourself standing in front of your seated form, so that it looks like your reflection in a mirror, then transferring your consciousness into this separated form. Contrary to what these writers say, this is not a necessary method to prove you are astral traveling. I know many people who astral travel and never see their own bodies.

Preparation for Astral Travel

Astral travel is an integrated part of your being (everyone astral travels during sleep). You should not fear it, but rather seek to remember and actively participate in it. The easiest

---

* Paracelsus. Trans. N. Guterman. *Selected Writings*. UK: Routledge & Kegan Paul, 1951.

and simplest method of astral travel comes about through deep meditation. Many people don't realize that they can use meditation in this way. To do so, prepare yourself as you usually would for a meditation, with phone shut off, in a place where you won't be disturbed, with soft background music to mask noise. Choose a comfortable chair, with arms if you feel you might fall over. I don't recommend lying down since that is a natural position for sleeping.

During any meditation or astral travel, you should begin by visualizing yourself completely surrounded by a brilliant white light for protection. This light also attracts positive entities and repels negative ones while you are out on the astral. The next step is to rid yourself of negative emotional baggage. One way of doing this is to visualize yourself standing beside a very deep well. Throw into this well all the negative thoughts, events, people, and problems with which you are dealing in life. This is a symbolic communication to the subconscious mind (which only speaks in symbols) that you wish solutions to these nagging problems.

The next procedure—relaxation of the total body—may take you some time to learn. Beginning with the feet and working up to the head, mentally tell each part of your body to relax. Spend extra time on the muscles of the shoulders, neck, and jaw, as these areas are most affected by tension and stress. Take as much time as you need to do this, but don't become tense from the work itself. As you relax the muscles in each area of your body, you will find your consciousness moving upward along with the relaxation. The relaxed portions of the body will feel heavy, if they have any feeling at all, while the consciousness feels very light. If the relaxation is done properly and the tension released, you will have no sensory input from the lower areas of your body by the time you reach your head. Your consciousness will feel as if it is no longer

attached to your body at all. In fact, as far as you are concerned, in the astral your body will convey no messages to you
at all, unless it is in danger.

Notice while astral traveling that colors appear more vivid
and your senses (which are now separated from the physical)
work at a heightened level. Your thinking processes are clear
and sharp; and while you may not be familiar with some of
the entities and places you see, never discount them.

Now is the time to direct your thoughts to a specific place
you wish to visit—usually an Otherworld level where you
meet with teachers and guides. This meeting place can be
anything you like: a Nature scene, an ancient temple, a beautiful garden, anything at all. Choose a place or scene in which
you feel comfortable, and as soon as you determine where
you want to go, you will be there. Since this book is about
astral love, you might consider furnishing this special place
with some kind of shelter—a cozy cabin, beach cabana, or a
bower. It is important that you decide where you want to go
before entering meditation. You certainly do not want to be
wandering aimlessly around the astral planes.

The following guided meditation will help you visualize
this special place in detail before you send out the call for an
astral lover. If you feel you aren't getting the results you
should, consider whether you are completely relaxed, expect-
ing instant results, or perhaps have unreasonable expectations.
Although you believe and expect that you can astral travel, at
the same time you have to be relaxed and ready to enjoy whatever you find. Don't ever fall into the trap of judging your
success by the amount of time you stay in meditation or astral
travel; time has absolutely no meaning on the astral planes. It
is quality, not quantity, which means the most. Whenever you
wish to return to your physical body, all you have to do is
think of returning and you will do so.

Meditation: The Meeting Place

Prepare as usual for meditation—phone shut off, pets out of the room, anyone else in the house warned not to disturb you, a comfortable chair, and soft non-vocal music. If you want to use candles and incense, be certain you set them far enough away that there is no danger of accidentally tipping over a candle or choking on incense smoke. Close your eyes and visualize the white light completely surrounding and protecting you. Take as much time as necessary to relax your physical body, but don't dwell on it and risk creating tension.

See yourself standing beside a deep well. Mentally gather up all the negatives in your life and drop them into the well. (This includes people.) Don't bother watching them fall, and walk away as soon as you have finished. Now think of the area in which you wish to build your meeting place—seaside, mountains, desert, forest, or by a lake. You can even visualize a place where two or more of these scenes are in close proximity. The choice is yours, since it will be your special place. As you stand in this place, make it come clearer to your mind by feeling the texture of any trees and flowers, smelling odors carried on the breeze, and listening for sounds of animals and birds. Stroll around your hideaway until you are familiar with it. It must be a place you enjoy, love to be in, and where you feel safe and comfortable. If there is something about it you don't like, change it. Also remember, this is *your* place; you have the right to exclude anyone—spirit or other astral traveler—whom you feel is trespassing without your consent. There is a group of entities known as the psychic police who will remove troublesome entities if you call upon their services. (For more on these police, see Chapter Four.)

Now is the time to begin building a shelter of some kind, a sort of vacation home. You do this by visualization. You can choose any type of architecture, large or small, although

I suggest something cozy. See the outside taking form, and when the outside is to your liking, enter the building and walk through the empty room or rooms. Begin the decorating by selecting colors for the walls of each room. Follow this with carpeting or polished wood or stone floors and draperies. Decide on the furnishings each room will have. If you've always wanted a certain style of furnishings and couldn't afford them in your everyday life, now is your opportunity to decorate to your heart's delight without worrying about the budget. Don't forget plants, pictures, a music source, and other details.

Since this place will reflect your true inner self, don't be surprised if it changes from time to time. As your emotional needs change, so will the furnishings and appearance of your special spot in the astral. If something changes which makes you uncomfortable, check to see if you are carrying negative emotional garbage into the astral with you. Your thoughts have a tremendous amount of creative energy, and that includes creating negatives.

When you are satisfied with the interior of the building, go back outside. Mentally call upon your guardian angels or spirit guides—whatever name you use to describe your personal teachers and protectors—to set up protective guards around this area. Turn clockwise toward each compass direction until you are aware of the protective boundaries which have been established.

Visualize a comfortable chair or bench outside where you can sit and watch the sunset or Nature. Sit there now as you wait for one of your teachers to appear, and the teacher will soon arrive. This may be one of your guides of whom you are already aware, or it may be someone new. Talk to the teacher about your desire to meet an astral lover. Since all communication on the astral is accomplished by telepathy, the more you relax and let the messages move freely between your minds, the easier communication will become. There are no language barriers in the astral.

The teacher will ask you to tell what you desire in an astral lover. I trust you will be concerned enough to go beyond looks, which are not the best indicator of positive character, as you should have learned from physical experience. Do you want gentleness, genuine concern for your well-being, true love and caring, or wisdom? For myself, I want an astral lover who will be all of these, plus be willing to help me accomplish my goals.

At the end of this conversation, the teacher leaves. You relax, feeling the healing spirit of your astral place soothing physical ailments and nervous tension from your body. When you wish to return to your physical body, simply think of it and you will be there. Don't jump up immediately. Open your eyes, stretch, and allow yourself time to readjust. If you stand up too quickly, you may get a headache or feel disoriented, possibly dizzy.

To prove to yourself that you were astral traveling, ask yourself the following questions: Were you totally unaware of your physical body and its surroundings while you were in the astral? Could you see, smell, and feel things? Were the colors vivid? Was your teacher real to you? Could you communicate with this teacher? If you can answer yes to most of these questions, then you were fully in the astral realm. If you had some difficulty, don't worry about it; the routine practice of meditation strengthens your ability to project into the astral. Never go into meditation with demands upon yourself to perform; this creates tension which keeps you from astral traveling. Don't make the mistake of judging your success by the amount of time you are in meditation or on the astral. There is no set amount of time which proves anything. There are no magick words which will instantly propel you to your goal; only self-discipline and practice will get you where you want to go.

Some people who find out about astral lovers want to contact a deceased loved one to continue a relationship. This is fine, provided you are being bluntly truthful with yourself about that person's past character and motives, and of course provided they want to participate in an astral relationship. We have all known couples who had miserable physical relationships, but as soon as one of them dies, the other constantly talks about their "wonderful character." When a person dies and goes onto the astral plane, they do not change; they are the same emotionally-tempered person they were in the physical. If your deceased lover tended to get violent, played around on you, hung out with bad company, lied to you, or anything else negative, you can count on the same behavior in the astral. Negative spirits are just waiting for an invitation into your aura, where they can cause all kinds of problems. So think carefully before you reestablish a relationship with a deceased person.

Since like attracts like, you need to take a good look at yourself and your own habits. If there is cleaning-up to do, do it before you call for an astral lover. You don't have to be perfect, but you had better be honest about yourself. Whenever you enter the astral plane, you always take with you all the emotions and ethics—positive and negative—which are clinging to your life. You also need to have some firm ideas about what you desire in an astral lover. You would not have a relationship with just anyone who was available in the physical;

the same applies to astral beings. You may not contract AIDS or venereal disease in the astral, but you certainly can catch their equivalent. This contamination occurs through the aura. Some psychics call it "psychic lice," an infestation which can do anything from creating negative events in your life to making you physically sick. If you do find yourself infected, clean your aura thoroughly (this is explained in detail in Chapter Five); then, take a good look at your behavior—physically and astrally—to see why you got into such a negative relationship in the first place.

At one time or another you will likely have a "bad trip." Discounting experiences under the influence of alcohol or drugs, this usually occurs because of negative emotional problems. If you don't believe that emotions influence your meditations and astral travel, just try going into meditation while under an emotional strain. Even if you think you have your negative emotions under control, there are times when they will transform into weird images in the astral. Emotional upheavals which generate negative thoughts and feelings also can draw to you low-level astral entities. Alcoholics and drug users often talk about the demon-like creatures who threaten them; these beings are attracted by low ethical and spiritual levels. In order to reach or stay on the higher astral levels and attract higher beings, you must be willing to make positive changes in your life and thinking wherever necessary.

Sometimes the emotions which cause astral distress are buried deep in the subconscious mind. You may have thought a problem had been taken care of long ago, but you never get rid of negative emotions by burying them and pretending they no longer exist. You have to drag them out into the light of day, acknowledge their existence, and begin dealing with them in a positive way. You and you alone are responsible for the kind of astral experiences you have. You may never run into many of the problems I've mentioned during your astral travels, but you certainly should know about them. This knowledge can help you understand the causes for variations in astral journeys and experiences. Don't be discouraged. Good astral experiences far outweigh the bad.

Another reason you may find yourself in the company of an unsavory entity is that your teachers have deliberately exposed you to such a creature to teach you how to discriminate on the astral plane. If this is the case, the teachers will not allow you in over your head; they will always be nearby, whatever the circumstances of your travels.

You can judge astral entities in much the same way you do when you meet physical people. Use common sense. Since your intuition is highly sensitized while in your astral body, be alert to how you feel when you meet an astral being. If this entity makes you uncomfortable or afraid, think yourself to another location. If necessary, end the journey. You have every right to choose who you want around you.

There is really no way you can truly believe in astral travel until you have experienced it for yourself. The only things you need are an open mind, an ability to see yourself truthfully, common sense, and a willingness to practice. Whether you ever get to the point of establishing a relationship with an astral being is not vital to your spiritual growth; there are lifetimes of learning to be had on the astral. Such a relationship is icing on the cake, but don't push yourself to experience such a relationship if you are uncomfortable with the idea.

Go to your special astral place often, until you look forward to spending relaxing time there. Use it as a weekend or evening vacation spot, a place to unwind and renew yourself. When you are ready spiritually, the astral lover will appear.

Two

∞

The Benefits
of Astral Love

By this time you might be kicking around the old ideas of *succubus* and *incubus* in association with an astral lover. Almost everyone has heard of these nasty entities who force themselves sexually on sleeping people. They do exist in the astral realm, just as rapists and unscrupulous and persuasive sex-hunters do in the physical world; however, these astral sex addicts have nothing to do with the authentic astral lover.

The words *succubus* and *incubus* do not specifically describe a low-level entity, but are definitions of astral lovers in general. Over the centuries, however, *succubus* and *incubus* have come to mean the low-level entities who come during sleep to force sexual intercourse upon unwilling humans. Since these descriptive words are now set in the human vocabulary to mean an undesirable astral entity, I will use that definition when speaking of such beings. *Incubus* is from a Latin word meaning "that which lies upon." This is a male astral entity who preys upon women. *Succubus* is from the Latin word which means "that which lies beneath." This is a female astral entity. The current definitions do not apply to an astral lover, who would never force intercourse or a relationship upon a human, whether in the physical or the astral.

If such an entity attempts to have sex with you while you are in your physical body, I guarantee it will not be your astral lover, but rather a low-level entity who still craves physical sex and doesn't care how he or she gets it. This astral sex addict is like the deceased alcoholic or drug addict—the craving and emotional demand are still there, and they don't care who they harm in their attempts to satisfy the craving. Reject this entity at once, before he or she can hook into your root chakra. If you think one has attached itself to your root center, take immediate action. Clean your aura (as described in Chapter Five); then consecrate and wear a protection amulet until you feel the danger is past. Check your emotions and thoughts to determine why you attracted such a being, if it was not by agreement. If it was by your agreement, decide why you agreed, and avoid engaging in astral lovemaking for at least six weeks. This deliberate abstinence will break any remaining connection.

There are a number of reasons why having a true astral lover is beneficial. For instance, there is no exposure to physical disease—an important consideration these days. Since one can't usually tell by observation whether a person has a contagious disease, it has become a form of Russian roulette to engage in physical sex. Even if you are acquainted with a person, the danger still exists; and marriage does not make you immune, if your mate should be engaging in questionable activities on the sly. Many spouses have gotten the unpleasant news that their mate has given them AIDS, venereal warts, drug-resistant venereal disease, or herpes. If you choose your astral lover carefully, there will be no danger of becoming infected with psychic diseases either.

If you yourself are infected with a deadly or contagious disease, you certainly do not want the negative karma of passing it on to another person. This leaves you in an emotionally unfulfilled state, without close affection and love from someone who really cares about you. Establishing a relationship with an astral lover can provide this caring, without exposing others to your disease.

If you are single and without a reliable partner, astral sex can be safe and fulfilling. Perhaps you had a negative experience and do not wish to be married, or remarried. Being content with an astral lover will remove you from the emotional pressure of conforming to the wishes of family, matchmakers, or orthodox religion, to put yourself on the marriage market.

A truly loving and concerned astral lover will also help you to meet a physical person who can share your life, if this is what you desire. An astral lover doesn't want you to live alone if you really want to have a physical companion. Your relationship with your astral lover will prepare you mentally and emotionally for the time when this "right" person comes into your physical life. You will have learned how to give of yourself and what to expect in return. The astral relationship will teach you to eliminate the desire to fall into the dependency trap—which so often occurs in physical relationships—when one person gives everything and the other only takes.

Suppose you have a mate or are married. You want a little spice in your life and aren't the kind of person who believes in cheating on your mate. Perhaps your present relationship has hit a rocky period where physical sex is non-existent or leaves something to be desired. An astral lover can lend emotional and spiritual support, satisfy your emotional needs, and perhaps influence the physical situation so that it turns for the better. This caring entity can also help you face reality if the physical relationship is bad for you or isn't going to get any better. Your astral lover can help you to disengage in a peaceful manner, protecting you if necessary. He or she will remain with you, teaching you how to recover your self-respect and dignity.

Just as your physical companion is your lover and friend on this plane of existence, your astral companion is your lover and friend on the astral plane only. A true, high-level astral lover will be much more tolerant of your physical relationship than your physical lover may be. An astral lover knows that the physical lasts only for so long, and then you must make the transition to the astral plane to await a new incarnation.

Having an astral lover is not cheating or sinful, even if orthodox religions would like you to think so. It is a fact that if you control a person's sex life you control the person. Such religions contradict themselves, for on one hand they say that such a relationship with an astral being is impossible, while on the other they rant about the sinfulness of such relationships. They do this because so much of the real knowledge about such relationships has been lost that they no longer know the truth—if they ever did. They also know that fear makes people easier to control, and that people fear what they do not know. Your knowing the truth about the astral and astral love would upset their control over your mind, and cause you to question their narrow vision of the afterlife.

Considering that the physical part of sex is actually the least important part of the experience, except for the production of children, emotion is what puts meaning and enjoyment into the sexual act. This ability to experience the romance, desire, excitement, and mystery of a relationship, and all the attendant emotions, are carried with you every time you journey into the astral. Without these emotions, there is nothing of value in the sexual experience, physical or astral.

Many astral lovers have been with you in other lifetimes, some from the very beginning of your existence as an individual soul. They are concerned about you and what happens to you. They care deeply about your spiritual progress, your happiness, your physical comfort. They are not only willing to provide you with emotional satisfaction while you are in the astral, but also will help you in reaching physical goals.

Preparing Yourself for an Astral Lover

As in physical life, you can get involved with the wrong lover if you are not careful, and are hasty in relationships. To draw the highest level of lover, you need to make certain preparations before sending out your signals. These preparations involve correcting and healing problems within yourself.

Begin by taking four sheets of paper. Label the top of each sheet with a title: Spiritual, Emotional, Mental, and Physical. On each sheet, list the things appropriate to that level which need work. Work on only one level at a time. Physical can include any health problems and bad habits. Mental includes such things as placing too much emphasis on the intellect relative to other areas of life, as well as manipulation and game playing. Emotional might include unreasonable outbursts of temper, unwarranted jealousy and resentments, or a habit of seeking revenge for every little thing. Old hatreds fall into this category. If you are still harboring the residue from events which happened years ago, find a way to release them. The Spiritual category might contain being closed-minded to new spiritual concepts, and a lack of common sense in using the ones you do believe in; the misuse of your spiritual beliefs; proselytizing to people who are not the least interested; or simply not taking time to work on your spiritual growth.

You need to be brutally honest with yourself; if you cheat, the only person you hurt will be you. What you are trying to do with this exercise is to rid yourself of as many negatives as possible before establishing an astral relationship. You will draw to yourself a level of astral being who matches your vibrations. For your own benefit, you should strive for the highest astral lover possible. (Heaven forbid you should want to wallow around with low-level entities!)

When you feel you have everything down on paper, begin physically doing what you can to correct as many faults as possible. Sooner or later, you will run into a mental barrier, where you find it impossible to get rid of something on your list. When this happens, you need to prepare for an astral-spiritual cleansing.

Cleansing the Physical

Before entering this meditation, read over the list you made of your physical problems. Go into meditation as described in Chapter One. Follow the meditation steps given; each step has a definite purpose. Return to the special astral place you created for yourself.

Choose an area within your special astral place for mentally constructing a small spiritual center or temple. Build it in any form you desire. Inside this structure, provide some type of altar and at least one comfortable chair in front of it. This temple can be simple or elaborate. You can add statues, candles, and whatever else appeals to you. Since this temple is a reflection of your spiritual side, don't be surprised if it changes in the future. As part of the actual temple, or at least very close by it, create a pool. This may be a spring, a stone-lined pool with steps down into it, a natural pool formed by a small waterfall dropping into it, or a calm inlet from the ocean.

Go back inside your temple and sit in the chair before the altar. Visualize your list of physical problems in your hands. Mentally review the things which you feel need to be corrected, and with which you have not had much success. Now lay the paper on the altar. If you are subconsciously hanging onto any of these physical problems, you may find that the paper sticks to your hands and you can't get rid of it. If this happens, there are two things you can do: either take it with you on the rest of this meditation or end the meditation and try to determine why you are subconsciously holding onto these things. You may find that part of the list will be released, but another part will tear free and stick to your fingers. Try to determine which of these "sticky" problems won't let go.

Now go to your sacred pool. Shed whatever garments you are wearing. If you still have the list, or part of it, stuck to your hands, don't worry. Call the white light around you. Slowly breathe in this light, feeling its tingling energy coursing through your body. When you feel ready, enter your sacred pool or stand under the waterfall. Release your physical problems to the healing energy of this water. Let the troubles be dissolved and washed away. At this point you may find that the list which was stuck to your fingers is dissolving as well.

As you leave the pool, stand in the warmth of the sun and feel the revitalizing energy making changes within your physical level. Although you must still be willing to make the effort to help the changes, believe that these changes will take place. Go back to the temple to say thank you before going on to spend whatever time you like in the rest of your special place. When you are ready to return to the physical, think of your physical body. Slide gently back into it and open your eyes.

Rather than destroy the list you made, keep it to help you realize when you are being healed. As each problem is taken care of, cross it off the list. Some problems may take longer,

but you will notice changes for the better. Note these
changes on the list.

Cleansing the Mental

Before entering this meditation, read over the list you made of
your mental problems. Go into meditation as described in
Chapter One. Return to the special astral place you created for
yourself. Take your list into the temple and sit in your chair.
Mentally review the items on the list, then lay the paper on the
altar. As with the physical cleansing, you may find that the list,
or part of it, will stick to your fingers. Try to determine which
mental troubles are creating this "sticky" situation. If the
paper is still attached to your hands, don't worry about it.

Go to your sacred pool. Call up the white light and visualize its brilliance all around you. Breathe it in slowly. Kneel
beside the pool and look at your reflection in the water. You
will notice a small whirling motion at the center of your forehead. This is what is called your third eye. Bring to mind one
of the mental problems on your list. Project this problem
through your third eye and let it fall into the water. As it falls,
reach out and push it under. Smooth the water with your
hands until all the ripples are gone and the surface is perfectly
smooth again. Repeat this with all the mental issues on your
list. Occasionally, you will find that one or more problems
will refuse to sink. You need to work harder on releasing
these issues. You may also find that one or more of the problems are difficult to force through your third eye. Don't give
up. Keep trying until they—and you—let go.

Wash your hands thoroughly in the pool. By this time,
even the part of the list stuck to your fingers will give up and
sink into the pool. Return briefly to your temple before going
out to enjoy your special astral place. When you are ready to

return to the physical plane, think of your body and slide gently back into it.

Cleansing the Emotional

Before entering this meditation, read over the list you made of your emotional problems. Go into meditation as described in Chapter One. Return to the special astral place you created for yourself. Upon entering your temple, decide where to put a mirror large enough to see your entire body. You may put it in the main temple area itself, or you may decide to create a small attached room. Near this mirror, create a comfortable table with overhead lights.

When you are finished with these additions, take your list and sit in your chair before the altar. Mentally review the items on the list. Emotional problems are some of the most difficult to detect or acknowledge; they often tend to hide their existence behind other issues. Take all the time you need to ferret them out. When you are satisfied that you are aware of at least the majority of them, lay the paper on the altar. Again, don't worry if some of the list sticks to your fingers.

Return to the mirror you created. Remove whatever garments you are wearing and stand before the mirror. This mirror is not the usual reflecting type, but one which shows only a silhouette of the entire physical body, outlined by the electrical energy produced by the emotional body. This mirror will show your emotional condition at any given time. Look carefully at the glow around your physical body. The longer you look, the more activity you will see in this fluctuating energy. Check the emotional body for flares, imperfect outlines, rippling effects, or dark areas. Try to determine which of the items on your list caused these. If you use your intuitive senses, you will very likely get a correct answer.

Lie down on your healing table underneath the lights. Relax and let go of any emotional feelings. The lights overhead will change to a soft blue color, bathing your body from head to foot. Breathe in this light; feel it soak into your emotional body, soothing and healing it. The lights change to a soft pink, again bathing you from head to foot. You feel loved and protected. Finally, the lights become a brilliant white, sealing any breaks in your aura, and filling you with a sense of well-being on all levels. You may now wander about your special place as long as you like before returning to the physical body.

Cleansing the Spiritual

Before entering this meditation, read over the list you made of your spiritual problems. Go into meditation as described in Chapter One. Return to the special astral place you created for yourself. Enter your specially created temple and sit quietly in your chair. Call upon the Goddess/God by whatever name you commonly use. Within a few moments, a brilliant oval of light will materialize before you.

Speak directly to this high-level being, explaining your efforts, or lack of them, in spiritual enlightenment and growth. Don't offer excuses because they usually will not be accepted. If your lack of spiritual growth has been through laziness, be truthful about it. You may receive a stern reprimand for such an attitude, but that is better than getting the full force of deity anger for not facing what you really are.

Listen to any answers given and consider them carefully. Too many people believe that everything told to them while in meditation must be swallowed whole. True spiritual messages are of great value, but never make drastic changes recommended by an astral being without using common sense. High-level spiritual beings never order or demand.

This deity will make contact with your vibrations, sending healing and positive energy into all your levels of being. Relax and enjoy the experience. Before leaving, She or He will give you a special pendant to wear. Although this astral pendant is invisible, it will remain with you wherever you go. Talk as long as you can with this deity, then enjoy the rest of your special astral place until you are ready to return to your physical body.

A word of caution here. Be extremely careful about believing astral messages if you are not good at looking at reality. You absolutely must see yourself as you really are, not some fantasy picture you have talked yourself into believing. Too often the answers heard in meditation are what a person wants to hear, not what is really being communicated. At one time, I was acquainted with a young man who "received" a message in meditation which told him he was the next Dalai Lama. Absolutely no one could convince him this wasn't true. What amazed me was that so many others thought he was a highly evolved spiritual person. Women flocked to him, and he had no compunction about using them and their money to make himself comfortable. Most of the so-called "spiritual information" he spouted was pure garbage. The last I heard, his wife had left him and he was drifting around with no purpose, living on whatever he could con out of people.

I assure you all this special cleansing of your bodies has not been a waste of time or a deviation from the subject of an astral lover. You should be striving to attract the highest-level astral lover possible, not settling for second best. The only way you can attract a high-level lover is to improve the conditions of your personal vibrations.

After a period of four or five months, you might want to redo your lists. This gives you an opportunity to see the progress you have made. Lots of times we are too hard on ourselves, always seeing only the things we have failed to do, not the things we have managed to accomplish. Periodic cleansing of your bodies also perks up your vitality and positive attitude toward life. It's very easy to become discouraged, low in energy, and depressed. Television, radio, newspapers, magazines, and movies add to this problem, rather than correcting it. Establishing a regular habit of returning to your special astral place is an excellent way to counteract all the negativity with which you are bombarded every day. Besides, one day you will enter your special place and find your astral lover waiting for you.

Enhancing Astral Travel

Sometimes we need a little help with astral travel, especially to heighten and sensitize the psychic sense we all have. Please don't turn to drugs; your astral travel will be out of your control, very probably propelling you into the lower levels. You also will not be able to end the travel when you want to; you will be locked in by the influence of the drug.

One of the easiest, and more pleasant, ways to aid astral travel and heighten psychic senses is through the use of herbs, stones, and oils. You can heighten your psychic sense for astral travel during sleep by using a dream-pillow, which is simple to make and non-toxic. Cut out two pieces of cloth about eight inches long by six inches wide. With the outsides of the two pieces together, stitch a narrow seam around three of the edges. Turn the bag right-side out. If you like decorated items, you can embroider any design of your choosing on the bag. Stuff with dried mugwort, an herb long known for its ability to enhance the psychic. Stitch the opening closed.

To use this dream-pillow, place it under your regular pillow when you go to bed, then go to sleep as usual. You will notice a definite sense-sharpness in dreams and nightly travels. Beware, however, that if you don't want to face the truth, don't sleep with a dream-pillow. You may well be presented with information—sometimes realistic, other times symbolic—which will have a direct bearing on your life. Either way, the training your astral body will gain while sleeping will be of benefit when you deliberately astral travel.

Stones

Using certain stones to help with deliberate astral travel, or while sleeping, is another safe method of enhancing and intensifying your experiences. These stones can be polished and set in jewelry, used tumbled smooth, or left in their natural state. Unpolished stones are just as powerful as the much more expensive polished ones. You can use more than one stone at a time, if you wish. If you choose to use a stone at night, put it under your pillow or wear it in a piece of jewelry. If your nightly astral excursions become too intense and make you uncomfortable, place the stone on the nightstand near the bed instead. The patterns of electrical energy pulses of your physical body and aura change from time to time. This may cause you to be comfortable with a stone one time, but uncomfortable with it a few months later. Use common sense and adjust the placement of the stone until you find a compromise. In a few months your energy pulses will likely readjust, and you can again use the stone at a close range.

The following list of stones are described according to their ancient uses. For more in-depth reading on stones and herbs, I consider any of Scott Cunningham's books the best there are.

Amethyst

The amethyst has been considered a high-vibrational, spiritual stone for centuries. Some writers associate this stone with the pineal gland, which would connect it with the brow chakra. Its violet color could also join it with the crown center. Magickally, it is excellent for spiritual journeying, and a valuable astral travel gem.

Aquamarine

This clear blue or blue-green gem was prized by seers and mystics. The ancients used aquamarine to reinforce psychic impressions and give clarity to mental visions. For astral travel, this gem aids in common sense and a clear mind.

Crystal, Quartz

This stone, sometimes referred to as rock crystal, is known to almost everyone. Crystals were sold by European apothecaries for healing purposes as late as 1750. Quartz crystal helps to open the psychic centers.

Lapis Lazuli

The spiritual significance of this stone was known to many ancient cultures from Egypt to Mexico. In astral travel, it aids in spiritual visions of a high nature.

Moonstone

I love moonstone, with its eye-like shimmer, and am including it for one very important reason: it helps to unmask enemies, whether on the physical or the astral planes.

Essential Oils

Essential oils have been used for as long as humans have known about them. Every essential oil has behind it a history of ancient magickal uses; and it is the tradition of many cultures that the scent of specific essential oils reacts on the psychic senses and light centers of the astral body.

Before using any oil on your body, place a tiny amount on the inside of your elbow to check for allergy and sensitivity. Some oils are highly toxic and irritating and should never be used on the body or in bath water. NEVER ingest oils! Smelling crushed herbs or fresh flowers can be substituted for some oils. The safest method of use is to put a drop or two of oil on a cotton ball, then place the cotton near your chair when you astral travel to your special place. Use one oil at a time, or you may get confused astral experiences.

Bay

Bay was sacred to the Delphi oracle in Greece. It promotes psychic awareness.

Calendula

I personally don't care for the fresh flowers, but the oil is said to produce psychic dreams.

Cinnamon

This oil causes extreme irritation if put on the skin; however, its odor can produce psychic awareness.

Deer's Tongue

A vanilla-scented herb, it is used by many readers of the tarot and runes to enhance psychic awareness. It can do the same for astral travel.

Frankincense

Don't use on the skin! The use of frankincense goes back at least three thousand years. It is said to make one more aware of spiritual realms, to reduce stress, and to release the conscious mind's control over the subconscious and superconscious minds.

Iris

The dried root of the Florentine iris is called orris root and smells like dusty violets. It strengthens the connection between the conscious mind and the psychic centers.

Lilac

Nowadays, the scent of lilac is said to drive away ghosts. Originally, it was used in ancient Mystery schools to promote far-memory, or recalling of past lives.

Mimosa

This oil encourages psychic dreams of the future and aids in understanding dream symbols.

Mugwort

This oil is hazardous! Use the plant instead. For centuries mugwort has been used by seers and mystics as an aid in divination. Its odor also promotes psychic dreams and astral travel.

Myrrh

The history of myrrh goes back as far as that of frankincense, if not farther. Its odor helps in meditation and enhancing one's awareness of the spiritual realms.

Sandalwood

Sandalwood is primarily imported from India. Sandalwood oil helps with meditation and raising one's spiritual vibrations.

Yarrow

This garden flower has a rich scent. Its odor helps to calm the conscious mind to the point where it allows psychic communication to take place.

Many of your astral experiences, at least in the beginning, may be cloaked in symbolism, because your conscious mind is trying to control the situation. You need to keep a journal of both deliberate astral travels and those experienced during sleep. By recording these "trips," no matter how bizarre they seem, you will begin to see a pattern in the symbols. By making your conscious mind look at the interpretation of the symbols, you can make it loose its hold and allow you greater freedom in your travels.

Now that you have taken positive steps to correct problems in all levels of your life, you are ready to send out a call to your astral lover. Proceed slowly, and enjoy the companionship you will find.

Three

Otherworld Lovers

aving a spirit lover is something which one must experience to fully understand. It is also one of the most controversial subjects about the astral. The belief in sexual intercourse between humans and astral entities has existed since before recorded history, and is a worldwide concept. Ancient peoples also believed it possible for children to be born from such relationships; however, even the ancients differentiated between astral lovers and astral sex-offenders.

In Greek mythology, there are several instances of astral relationships—some good, some bad. Since many of the myths were rewritten after the takeover by the patriarchal clans, there is no way to determine if the original stories were, in fact, of astral lovers and their human loves. Some of the stories of these Greek "gods" tell of Otherworld entities who cared for their human lovers and the children produced from the relationship; these can be construed to be true astral lovers. Other "gods," however, were obviously astral rapists and nothing more. The ancient Greeks called the offspring of these unions, demigods. Some of them never assumed human form, while others were totally human. Generally speaking, there were three types of "children" produced by astral relationships: a "physical child," an "astral child," and a magickal-physical manifestation. These "children" are often called "magickal children." The subject of the "magickal child" is discussed in Chapter Nine.

In Norse mythology, the god Heimdall is called the father of the three human races. As Heimdall traveled about, he spent three nights as the guest of three different families. Each night he had sexual intercourse with the wife of that particular family. The son born to each of the three women was considered to be the progenitor of one of the three races: Karls, Jarls, and Thralls.

Although most of the stories about the Norse goddess Freyja were destroyed by Christian monks, there is a surviving tale which tells how she cavorted with Otter, a human man. Since the Giantess Hyndla calls Freyja a rutting she-goat, I scarcely think "cavorting" means dancing in the moonlight.

The Celts of Ireland have stories of humans and immortals loving each other, and, on rare occasions, producing children. In Scotland, these astral lovers were known as the Leannain Sith—faery lovers or familiar spirits. Like the Irish, the Scots relegated the Old Gods to the position of faeries after Christianity took over. The practice of astral sex must have been common, for Robert Kirk, a clergyman writing in a book on faeries in 1690 or 1691, warned against the practice. Kirk calls these female entities paramours and strumpets, saying that many young men willingly cohabited with them. He also writes that both men and women could have faery lovers, with the women sometimes bearing a physical child of the union. However, as a Christian minister, Kirk had some very prejudiced statements to make about the practice.

Geoffrey of Monmouth also wrote of such astral relationships. He states that the famous sorcerer Merlin came from such a union of a mortal woman and a faery man. Geoffrey called these entities *daemones,* meaning "familiar spirits," the same term used much earlier by the Greek philosopher Pythagoras. When Christianity, Islam, and Judaism gained control, astral rapists and lovers were lumped together and called evil demons.

In shamanic traditions, the practice of sexual intercourse with a spirit entity was accepted as a common experience of the shaman, and was, in fact, the mark of a powerful shaman. Shamans frequently speak of having astral wives or husbands by whom they have children. These children are raised in the Otherworlds by the astral parent, and are never mentioned as having any physical form. Children remaining in the Otherworlds is a more common theme in cultural belief than that of children being born mortal.

A few magickal traditions appear to have used the astral lover as a substitute for human sex. The remaining records list only female participants, which is hardly surprising since the orthodox religions are always telling people how "evil" women are and how they should be under a man's control and domination. (To be fair, there were probably men who practiced this, too.) Today in Mexico there are still certain female "witches" who use an unguent called *toloachi*, which they say enables them to contact their spirit lovers. This unguent contains deadly herbs, much as did the flying ointments of the medieval Witches. These women are said to have no need for men, something considered extremely sinful by both the men and the churches.

Please DON'T use drugs or any "flying ointments" to make contact with your astral lover. Many ingredients in these ointments are deadly, and drugs and ointments are only likely to project you into the dangerous lower levels of the astral planes, where you will have to contend with criminal spirits. If you don't care how you get your astral sex, you will get what you deserve, and it will not be a pleasant experience. You will find that you have opened yourself to the advances and misuse of any low-level entity who comes along. In short, you will become a free prostitute for the worst kind of astral beings.

Recognizing an Astral Lover

To be doubly sure you are not dealing with some unscrupulous entity, insist upon a courtship period before agreeing to engage in anything more than talk and companionship. Take your time getting acquainted with your astral lover. Spend quality time expressing your thoughts and feelings. Engage in a little hugging and kissing, and just feeling loved and cared for. If this being insists upon or keeps suggesting something more, you have every right to be offended. If some strange human approached you and suggested having sex, you would probably report him or her to the police. The very least you would do would be to get away from that person as fast as you could. You use the same tactics in the astral. In fact, there are astral "police" whom you can call. (There is more about these protectors in Chapter Four.) Knowing this, you may be reluctant to search for an astral lover, but there is no reason to be apprehensive. If you keep your ethics and goals high, your vibrations and thought-patterns will not attract low-level astral entities.

The astral lover is a being who is as loving and concerned about you as any true physical lover should be. By astral lover, I am not speaking of just any astral being who shows an interest in you. You would never have a sexual experience with just anyone who shows an interest in the physical, so there is no reason to act so irresponsibly in the astral. A true astral lover is a being who has loved you from before the time you were born into this life, and probably has loved you for centuries of lifetimes. Sometimes, in your long succession of lives, the two of you existed in physical form. Sometimes only one of you was in the physical while the other watched from the astral realms. The love you felt for each other continued even though you had to meet and touch only on the astral planes. This astral lover is waiting for you to acknowledge his or her existence, ready and eager to help you in any way possible. As with anyone who truly loves another person, the astral lover wants to do more than make love. This wonderful relationship can be renewed during your astral travels, whether the traveling is done during sleep or deliberately. An astral relationship can have all the same tenderness, warmth, and satisfaction of a physical one, and because your senses intensify while in the astral, you will discover new and enhanced feelings.

It is quite natural to be fearful about making contact with this astral lover and feeling his or her touch. When you move to the next stage of your development, you will probably worry that you *won't* make contact. Fear and tension keep you from having a positive astral experience; in fact, they will probably keep you from astral traveling at all. So try to put yourself in the position of joyfully awaiting this new experience, while at the same time not feeling as if you are a failure if it doesn't happen right away.

Now that you are cleansed and aware of yourself and the possibilities of the astral, you are ready to prepare yourself for an actual meeting with your astral lover. Before you arrange for this meeting, however, you should determine what qualities you desire in this being. The following brief test will help you to be more exact in projecting your desires.

1. Which of the following qualities have meaning for
    you in your choice of companions? Number them in
    the order of their importance:

    > *gentleness*
    > *compassion*
    > *concern*
    > *tenderness in loving*
    > *intelligence*
    > *sense of self-worth*
    > *decisiveness*
    > *willingness to protect*
    > *spiritual advancement*
    > *understanding for physical life and its trials*
    > *truthfulness*
    > *healing ability*
    > *progression on the Otherworld levels*
    > *patience*

    If you think of any others, add them to your list.

2. Do you have a particular past incarnation from which
    you might want the lover to be? Be careful here, for by
    being too exact you may exclude an astral being who
    would be more compatible; and there is the possibility
    that a person who was compatible during one lifetime
    will not be compatible in another. It always makes me
    uneasy when anyone declares they have found their
    soulmate—even on the astral planes. Personalities
    change through life experiences; therefore, no being
    remains the same, life after life. (Attracting more than
    one spirit lover is discussed in Chapter Seven.)

3. What are your goals in life? List them in their order of
    importance.

Perhaps the idea of an astral relationship including sex strikes you as impossible. Think carefully about your past astral experiences in both meditation and dreams. Didn't you feel the touch of your teacher-guide? Couldn't you feel emotions when you reviewed a past life? Don't block yourself from this new experience because you might be frightened or turned off by the word, sex. Some physical relationships endure without any sexual connotations; if this is your desire, you can keep your astral loving at this level. You never have to jump into sex with anyone, here or out there. Set your parameters and go at your own speed.

Before following the guided meditation to reach your astral lover, you should be aware of all the possibilities to expect. In seeking and being with an astral lover, you have to take care in how you exit from your physical body to not attract the attention of any low-level entities. The chakra through which you exit for this astral journey should be carefully considered. Always avoid the lower three chakras. Leaving through the first two is a sure ticket to the lower astral levels, and the third, the solar plexus center, will tie you into pure emotions. By using the third light center you may open up communications with deceased spirits who once had an emotional bond with you. This may or may not be pleasant. You really want to exit through a higher center so you can make a more spiritual connection. After all, this relationship should be a highly spiritual experience. Exiting through the heart chakra will connect you to past true loves; the throat chakra reestablishes contact with lovers who may be more intellectual in nature. By using the brow or crown chakras as exit points when visiting your astral lover, you can be sure to avoid attracting low-level entities, and won't end up somewhere on the lower astral planes fighting off perverts.

If you have difficulty pulling your consciousness out of the physical body as you separate the astral from the physical, try visualizing a tornado of swirling energy, point down at the top of your head. Let this tornado lift you up out of the body. You still will have the cord connection and the ability to return whenever you wish.

Before embarking on your astral journey, tune your thoughts to those of love, companionship, and a true lover. Prepare yourself as if you were going out on a date. You might even arrange your altar or a table in your ritual area with a pink candle and some flowers. All this may arouse your physical lover, and, if so, enjoy the experience. In fact, the physical loving may make it easier for you to open your emotions and psychic senses to your astral lover. A positive astral lover will never be jealous of your physical relationships with your present spouse or lover. A genuinely concerned astral lover will not want you to be alone during this physical existence, if you desire companionship. He or she will be happy when you are happy, and feel compassion when you are depressed or sad. This being will help you in any way possible to improve your life, health, and spiritual enlightenment, all without demanding anything in return. Your spirit lover will always work for your benefit, give you good advice, alert you to upcoming problems, and help to heal you when you are sick. He or she can provide you with information, aid you in astral traveling, and guide you in seeing and taking advantage of opportunities to better your life.

If you have just experienced a negative emotional event, postpone the astral journey. Your emotional reaction to the physical happening will only mar your journey. Give your emotional body time to readjust itself so you won't be sending out negative signals in the astral. Like attracts like, and you don't want to attract an undesirable entity.

Finding Your Astral Lover

Be sure you pull your consciousness up to at least the brow chakra before you go out onto the astral. Once there, send out your call for your astral lover. You will likely be surprised to find him or her already waiting for you; connections from past lives together will have made such a strong bond between the two of you that an instant's thought will bring you together. If your astral lover doesn't immediately materialize beside you, don't worry; he or she may choose to come to you later in your special place.

Upon meeting, spend a few minutes looking at your lover. Notice the color of the hair and eyes, the contours of the face, what nationality he or she has chosen to represent. At the first remembered meeting, the astral lover will probably assume the features and clothing of a past life which had great meaning for both of you. This may help you to subconsciously recall memories from that time period. Feel the loving touch as you clasp hands. You may even be gathered into a loving embrace, which will fill you with intense joy. Ask for a name.

Your lover may suggest that the two of you go to the temple where the Akashic records are kept. I assure you this will be an enlightening experience. If you had difficulty reading or understanding your Akashic records before, this is a wonderful opportunity to look at them with an interpreter by your side. Your lover will at first choose those lifetimes which involved the two of you; however, at later times he or she will help you to see and understand other lifetimes you wish to explore. Sooner or later, you will discover it is possible to look into the Akashic records of other people, but don't become a snooping busy-body! It is perfectly ethical to look into the records of people who have a direct bearing on your life, if you seem to be having difficulties with them. It can also be vital to look into the records of anyone who is not close to you but who is creating problems for you, such as troublesome neighbors or business associates. You may well discover an unresolved problem between these people and you; or you may simply find they have a long history of negative behavior.

Spend several astral journeys getting to know your lover. He or she may take you to interesting places for visits in the astral planes themselves, to present-time locations, or forward and backward through time itself. If you have experienced difficulty contacting the spirit of a deceased loved one, your astral lover will do everything possible to arrange a meeting. Not only that, the lover will be a guardian for the entire time you are out on the astral planes. Never be afraid to ask your astral lover for help with a problem or in improving your life (materially or otherwise). Like anyone who truly loves, this being will help all he or she can. In return, don't talk to others about your astral love life, for this can expose your lover to hate and ridicule. This may mean not telling your physical lover or spouse about your astral relationship, especially if you have a mate who would not understand. Why create unnecessary trouble when the second relationship is actually a spiritual one?

As with all lovers, at some point, you will want to do something nice in return. An astral lover might suggest a repayment in the form of working to heal or help another person—physical or astral. Remember to use your common sense when considering such a suggestion. If the astral lover is truly working for your benefit, he or she will never suggest anything that is wrong, harmful, or against your code of ethics. Many people have a bad habit of accepting everything told to them on the astral as something they should implement immediately or accept without question. Remember, spiritual entities do not look at things the way we do in the physical. Some of what you hear might not be true, but rather just what you want to hear. Spirit lovers can be just as free with compliments as are physical lovers. If your astral lover says you were someone famous in another life, take it as a compliment only, not as fact. Lovers often say such things to each other, never meaning for them to be taken literally. It is just an expression of love.

Ritual to Prepare for Your Astral Lover

It is best to perform this ritual in a place where you will not be disturbed or eavesdropped upon. This is especially important if you want to talk to your astral lover.

Prepare a small altar with the following tools: a white candle in a fireproof holder; lotus, rose, or jasmine oil; lotus or frankincense incense (sticks or cones); a chalice or glass of fresh water; a chalice or glass of wine, juice, or soda; a standing mirror; and a towel on which to clean your hands. Have a comfortable chair in which you can sit close to the altar.

If you wish, you can perform this ritual within a cast and consecrated circle; however, this is not absolutely necessary. Light the incense and fan the smoke throughout the area, as well as over yourself. Place the mirror in the center of the altar with the candle on the right side, the incense on the left. Put a small amount of the oil into the palm of your power hand (the hand with which you write); and slowly stroke the candle with this oiled hand, applying the oil from the candle wick to the bottom. As you do this, think about meeting your astral lover. Mentally (or aloud) invite this being to join you at your altar. Set the candle in the holder and clean your hands. Hold your power hand over the glass of water and say:

> *By the power of the Goddess/God, with the aid of*
> *my teachers and my astral lover, through the*
> *cosmic energy which flows through my body, this*
> *water is blessed.*

Lightly sprinkle the water around the altar, moving in a clockwise direction. Dim the lighting in the room and sit in your chair. Say:

> *I send an invitation into the astral planes to my*
> *perfect astral lover. Please join me here at this*
> *altar that we may become better acquainted.*

Light the candle. Raise the chalice of juice in a salute, then slowly sip it. Look deeply into the mirror at your reflection and say:

> *Let me feel your presence. Help me to recognize*
> *you, for so much time has passed since I was last*
> *aware of your existence.*

Relax, sip the juice, and gaze into the mirror as if it held the reflection of your astral lover. In your own words, talk to this centuries-old companion, expressing any hopes or fears just as you might with an extremely close friend. Take as much time as you feel you need for this part of the ritual. If you are blessed with seeing your reflection alter into a slightly different form in the mirror, don't panic; your astral lover will be showing you how you looked in other incarnations. To prove his or her presence, you may feel a pat on the head, a feathery embrace, a light kiss. You may even suddenly experience a sense of being deeply loved. Sometimes the presence of astral beings is experienced as the sensation of cobwebs brushing around your face or something moving your hair.

Your automatic response will be to brush your hand across your face or over your hair. When you discover that nothing physical is there, you can relax and begin to really understand contact with astral beings.

Continue to talk and drink the juice as long as you wish. When you are ready to end the meeting, bid your astral lover good-bye. Ritually open the circle (if you cast one), but leave the candle in a safe place to burn completely out.

This ritual is like a hand-written invitation to your astral lover, notifying him/her that you are ready and willing to make contact. It is also your first tentative step to becoming comfortable with the decision you've made to renew the relationship. When you feel you are really prepared to meet and see your astral lover, proceed with the following meditation-astral travel.

Meditation: Meeting Your Astral Lover

Go into meditation in your usual manner, remembering to surround yourself with white light and to dump your negative problems. As soon as you are totally relaxed and have lifted your consciousness up at least to the brow chakra in the center of your forehead, visualize yourself in the special astral place which you built.

Prepare yourself for meeting with your astral lover. Dress yourself in any type of garment (or no garments), whatever you wish. You might want to relax for a few minutes in the pool near or within your sacred temple area. It will be quite normal to feel some flutters of anxiety and anticipation, but stay as relaxed as possible; after all, you will be meeting someone who will have, and probably already has had, an important influence upon your life. Think of your astral lover, who will at once be standing beside you. Look deeply into his or her eyes (for it is not by chance that the eyes are called the "windows of the soul"). Allow yourself to become aware of his or her physical looks, any clothing or apparel, the sound of his or her voice. Smile and say how happy you are to finally become aware of your lover. (Remember, all conversations on the astral planes are by instant telepathic communications from one mind to another. There is no language barrier.)

Your astral lover may decide to take you to visit somewhere special, perhaps a place or time which held deep meaning for the two of you. You may begin this trip with a stop at the temple of Akashic records where you will be able to view portions of your past lives together. Relax and enjoy the companionship of this astral being, and remember, you never have to engage in more than hand-holding if that's what you want.

At some point in this meeting, your lover will ask you about your present life, what help he or she can give to make it better. This being may also introduce you to teacher-guides of whom you were not yet aware. If you want to contact a deceased friend or loved one, your astral lover will help you to do this, and he or she will be your protector all the time you are out on the astral planes.

When you are ready to end this astral-meditation, say good-bye and think of your physical body. You will feel your lover's hands helping you to return.

Meet several times with your astral lover so you can get acquainted with his or her vibrations and recognize them whenever he or she is near. Become comfortable with, and trusting of, your astral lover before you engage in the sexual chakra melding. As always, if this act makes you uncomfortable, you need never do it; the choice is always yours. A true astral lover will never nag or try to force you into anything you don't want to do.

Loving on the Astral Planes

Eventually there will come a time when you wish to express your joy and love in other ways than just an embrace or a warm kiss. Astral love with a higher astral being is a bona fide spiritual experience, and is not evil, sinful, or dirty. Orthodox religions do not want you to know the truth behind this ancient secret, for it sets you free from their control. You become your own, independent person.

Don't expect astral sex to be like physical sex; it isn't. Your astral lover will be gentle, guiding you into the astral experience with great tenderness. No one can give you more than the basics of what to expect; there is just no way to express the intensity and beauty of the experience. You will stand or lie face to face with your spirit lover. You will feel your throat center begin to increase in size, helping to clear all the chakras by removing obstructions. This expansion increases your creativity, intensifies your psychic talents, and helps you to be more physically articulate. Even without all these side benefits, this enlarged throat center produces an almost sexual tingling throughout your astral body. (An interesting point is that this same technique can be used with your physical lover if he or she believes as you do, and understands about the chakras and energy exchange.)

As both your chakras align, a form of light-center intercourse begins. All higher-level astral entities begin the exchange of energy from at least the brow chakra, moving up to the crown chakra and then moving down through the rest of the light centers. This exchange of etheric energy is a fantastic experience which makes physical sex seem very juvenile. On occasion, this astral intercourse will produce a corresponding sexual reaction in the physical body. If you are astral traveling while asleep, you may experience an orgasm; or you may find yourself coming out of a deliberate astral journey in a very sexy mood.

Acknowledging your personal astral lover, and choosing to spend time with him or her, can definitely help with your development and progress, both in astral travel and spiritual growth. With your lover's help you can improve your material life, get better results with your magick and healing, and have an excellent warning system against psychic attacks or upcoming negative physical events. Be realistic about your astral lovemaking. Don't lose yourself to loving on the astral plane exclusive of everyday life and physical relationships. Such an attitude and behavior will create an imbalance in your aura and will cause problems. Some people get so carried away with the idea and experiences of meditation, for instance, that they become almost non-functioning humans living in some self-created dream world.

The astral lover can be friend, advisor, teacher, protector, and lover, all rolled into one being. He or she can take you to spiritual teachers who can reveal long-forgotten mystical knowledge. You need never feel alone and despondent again. Your own special lover-friend is only a thought away. This special beautiful relationship has endured for centuries and can keep on enduring for centuries more. Your astral lover was there with you as you awaited your birth into this world, and will be waiting when you leave this physical plane to once more return to the spirit realms.

Four

∞

The Good,
the Not-So-Good,
and the Slimy

There is a wide diversity of astral travel experiences. You can't experience astral travel in a positive way unless you keep an open mind, change your life into a positive mode, and are prepared to believe your experiences while using common sense. There are no exact maps to the astral planes, just general descriptions shared by travelers. These descriptions of what and who are where are much the same, and should be closely observed in order to stay out of trouble.

The Astral Levels

Traditionally, the astral plane is said to be made of seven levels, with a very high, inaccessible level above these seven. When speaking of the astral levels, the words, higher and lower, have nothing to do with social classes, outward appearance while on Earth, what church you did or didn't go

53

to, or the amount of time spent in worship. Rather, these terms indicate areas of existence inhabited by evolved or devolved souls. A human spirit earns its place on a particular level by its actions and deeds in its past earthly life. True spiritual seeking—not the outward pretense—also helps determine to which level a spirit is assigned. Entities and spirits which never were human also dwell on levels which correspond to their vibrations. This division according to spiritual vibrations is one of the real manifestations of karma.

The first, and very lowest, level is inhabited by all the slimy nasties of the astral planes. This lower level is like a combination of crime-ridden ghetto slums, state penitentiary, and mental ward. Here are vast areas of chaos, unstable emotional energies, evil, and danger, often referred to as a plane of darkness. This does not mean beings on this level can't see or be seen (as one couldn't see in a darkened room), but describes a level of spiritual darkness. Although human spirits may be confined to this level, even for several lifetimes, it is not a place of perpetual punishment and torture as described by orthodox religions. A spirit can work to raise its spiritual and ethical life and thus be released from this plane. Unfortunately, as with Earth-plane prisons, most of the inhabitants simply don't want to change their ways.

The five intermediate astral levels range from what might be called beginner to advanced. These are the astral levels you actively seek in your travels. It is on these levels that you want to look for your astral lover, seek teacher-guides, and learn from the inhabitants. You will seldom, if ever, be threatened on these levels, but can expect to be protected and guided to the exact place, class, or teacher who will be of the most help to you.

The highest of the seven levels is the dwelling place of what we call deities. The powerful inhabitants of the seventh level are the energy forms that Jung referred to as "arche-types." The only way you will be able to travel to this level is if your spiritual thoughts match the vibrations there, if the deities themselves take you there personally, and if you are not harboring negative emotions and intentions.

The level above this seventh level is never entered by humans, either in the spiritual or astral body, for this level is the dwelling place of the Supreme Creator/Creatrix behind the Gods. This unfathomable power source may on rare occa-sions project a tiny portion of its power and presence to a human, but the usual method of communication (if there is any with humans) is through special messengers. And, no, this powerful being is not the Christian god, regardless of the claims orthodox religions make.

The Types of Astral Beings

Whether you are seeking your astral lover or just traveling about on the astral planes, there are a number of different types of astral beings who may approach you. Even if you should be fortunate enough to never encounter the negative ones, you should be aware of their existence, what they are like, and how to handle them if you meet them. The biggest concern of new astral travelers is "How do I know if an entity is positive or negative?" This is a legitimate concern, since the astral planes have all kinds of beings, just as there are all kinds of humans here on Earth. Besides low-level entities, deity forms, teachers, discarnate acquaintances, and other astral travelers, you can meet elves, faeries, other Nature spir-its, and human-created thoughtforms. On infrequent occa-sions, you might meet with the powerful Goddess (Maiden, Mother, Crone) or the God, perhaps as Lord of the Forests and Animals. These deities will most often take the form you relate to in your spiritual studies. The Goddess and the God are really archetypal energy sources, not confined to one religious belief or form, and answering to thousands of names.

You need to judge character of spiritual entities in the same way you do when you meet people in the physical. Use your intuition and common sense! When you meet an astral being, your first impression is generally accurate. Be aware of how you feel about them. Your intuitive senses are highly sharpened in the astral and can be trained to be quite reliable. If something about an astral entity makes you uneasy, move yourself to another area. If necessary, end the astral journey. You have every right to choose who you want around you, both in the physical and in the astral.

The easiest method of deciding the polarity of an astral being is through the aura. All astral entities and spirit beings have auras, just as physical humans and human astral travelers do. Look closely at these auras to determine what the colors and possible symbols mean to you. Open your intuitive senses. Are you comfortable, uncomfortable, or do you want to get away as fast as you can? When the aura of an astral or physical being makes contact with your own aura in the physical, you immediately sense that you are not alone, even if you can't see the person. When you are out on the astral, you can see these auras as well as feel the true emotional intentions coming from them. Watch for the clarity of colors, and the colors themselves, around all entities.

Don't ever assume you automatically know who an astral being is; appearances can be deceiving. This applies to deities as well as other entities, who will tell you who and what they are if you ask. Don't fall for the erroneous idea that calling a negative entity by its name will compel it to do good; all beings, astral or physical, are true to their nature. If they are negative, nothing you do or say will compel them to be otherwise. If you have the feeling that you are being followed in the astral by something which makes your skin crawl, but you can't identify the being which makes you feel this way, order it to allow you to see it. Astral creatures and beings must appear if challenged. Thoughtforms (built by physical humans and some other astral travelers) will try to avoid this confrontation, but eventually must appear if you keep repeating the challenge.

Since all humans astral travel automatically when they sleep, and some can deliberately astral travel whenever they wish, it is inevitable that you will encounter human travelers on your journeys. The vast majority of these are benign, but, on occasion, you may meet a "nasty" (its true form still on the Earth plane in a physical body) who is out on the astral preying on unwary travelers. Treat them as you would any negative astral entity. Call on the astral police to take it away. Call on your teachers to help protect you until the annoying creature is gone. Try to avoid touching any such negative creature or thoughtform, or its aura. Contact between auras on the astral is like giving your address and phone number to a thief or rapist; sooner or later you can expect to find them in your home.

Anne was what I call a fence-sitting pseudo-Pagan. She didn't want to totally give up her orthodox religion, but still wanted to do magick and develop her psychic talents. She also believed that love could conquer anything; that if you expressed love to any person or astral creature you could change it into something good. When Anne mentioned that she was astral traveling to "save souls" on the astral planes, several people warned her not to take such an attitude or she would get into trouble. She wouldn't listen. We noticed that she soon had a haggard look about her, but she said nothing for several weeks.

One afternoon Anne appeared at my door in hysterics. Her life was falling apart. She saw hideous faces and heard demonic voices constantly in her mind; her dreams were filled with nightmarish creatures. Her aura was terrible and filled with psychic lice as well as having several attached auric threads. It didn't take long to determine that she was accompanied by three very negative astral entities. I cleansed her aura as best I could, and told her to give up astral traveling for a long while. When I asked her what she had been doing, she replied, "Saving souls on the lower astral planes. I hug them and tell them how much they are loved. That is my god-given mission in life." She refused to listen to anything I said about staying away from such astral creatures. She continued her "work," and her mental state continued to go downhill. Finally, she joined a radical orthodox group who performed exorcisms for every rash or pimple, and who told her (of course) that, with her prayers, she was doing great work for god. The last I heard her life was worse than ever.

Deliberate and Subconscious Thoughtforms

If you encounter a thoughtform created by another human, you must decide whether the sending was done consciously or subconsciously. If the thoughtform was consciously created and sent to you, drive it back to the sender by visualizing a shaft of white light pushing it away. You don't have to know who sent it; thoughtforms always know the way back to their maker. (Remember this if you should decide to create an astral thoughtform to harass someone.) Never specify what you want to happen to the sender; this will lock you into their troubles. Deliberately created thoughtforms are much more aggressive than those subconsciously formed, and sometimes must be compelled with forceful words and actions; however, don't feel a doormat obligation to be nice to these deliberately created, annoying thoughtforms. One should never be nice to an astral stalker.

If the thoughtform was subconsciously created, try to discover what emotions and events caused it, and who is responsible. You may be surprised to find out that their creator is someone close to you. Some of them may even be your own creations. Obviously you do not want to harm yourself or someone who is not deliberately causing you trouble. With your teachers' help, encircle the offending thoughtform with white light, then concentrate on changing its power from negative to positive.

If you think the idea of giving life to thoughtforms is ridiculous, think again. Thoughts, as with all creations, are made of energy. The electrical impulses (thoughts) of the brain are a form of energy. Every time you think or visualize, you are putting out energy pulses. Fortunately, the majority of our thoughtforms are short-lived. The thoughtforms which exist for longer periods of time are those in which we invest a large amount of emotion and mental visualization.

Many of the powerful thoughtforms roving around the astral planes have been created by more than one person. The same thoughts or imaged ideals held by many people (especially over many years) will eventually create a corresponding, powerful entity in the astral. This image ideal becomes a living creature on the astral—for good or ill. The Christian devil is a prime example of this type of creation, as are the saints. These are two extremes in vibrations created by the same general religious ideas.

The astral plane is very sensitive to thoughts and emotions beyond the creation process. Humans are constantly producing emotional thoughts such as fear, anger, hate, love, desire, and intense spirituality. Thoughts are triggered by emotions—some weak, some strong. These emotional thoughts send out waves of vibrations, attracting astral entities of like vibrations. Constantly fearing something, for example, provides a steady stream of energy which will attract negative thoughtforms or entities into your life. Denying your fear, if you still actually fear it, is not getting rid of the energy flow; you have to replace the negative thought with a positive one. For instance, if you believe in reincarnation and a cognizant afterlife, there is no longer any reason to fear death. If you are a Pagan and realize that the Christian devil is a creation of that religion, then you can convince your subconscious mind that, for you at least, this being has no validity or power.

If you encounter a negative thoughtform or astral being, stand your ground. Face the entity, but try to stay away from its aura. Don't let its projected emotion of fear get to you. These types of beings feed and grow on the fear they cause you to feel. Instead, shout at them! Both thoughts of sound and vocalized sound, even on the astral, create vibrations. The vibrations of a shout (even a mental one) are strong enough to forcefully carry such an entity away from you. Tell it in no uncertain terms that you don't believe in it. Disbelief and laughter are two of the best weapons a person can use on any plane of existence.

Another method of defense is the circle of flame. Before going out onto the astral, visualize yourself completely surrounded by a ring of white fire. This ring will automatically move with you, so you need never fear losing it. To create a ring of fire, mentally draw the circle around yourself with the forefinger of your power hand, moving clockwise. Overlap the ends to seal it. No astral entity or thoughtform can cross this flame circle unless you let it in.

If you forgot to draw the circle before your travels and an annoying astral entity surprises you, take quick action by calling up a ball of brilliant white light, surrounding yourself with it instantly. Then create more balls of light and hurl them at the solar plexus area of the offending entity. This causes a scrambling of any emotional hook-up it is attempting with you. Keep throwing balls of light until the entity retreats in total confusion, which it eventually will. This works whether the entity is an astral creature, an astral projection of another person, or a thoughtform. This white light causes immediate discomfort and often pain to low-level entities, regardless of how nice they represent themselves to be.

If you suspect the offending creature is an astral projection of another person, also throw balls of light directly at the center of their forehead to "blind" them. The psychic third eye is the seeing mechanism used while in the astral body. Blinding this center with light prevents your attacker from seeing where you go or what you do next. If an entity should actually hook into your astral body (they will try for the lower three chakras), immediately and violently chop down on the offending appendage with your hand, while seeing your whole body as living white fire. Kick out sharply with your foot to the knee or groin area (root center). Smack the heel of your hand into the third eye (brow chakra). Punch the solar plexus. These astral forms of judo are very effective. While you are defending yourself, don't overlook the power of the astral voice. Shout at the entity; do it with great indignation that anyone or anything should dare lay hands on you.

When on the astral, actions happen as soon as you think of them. Keep the intellect out of it when an emergency arises, and rely on your intuitive reactions. Falling back on the left brain intellect will cause you to reason everything to the point of immobilizing yourself. While traveling in the astral, develop an attitude of "don't even think of bothering or threatening me!" Astral entities, like physical attackers, usually prey on those they feel are afraid or timid. Ordinarily, having this attitude is enough to deter all but the most determined of negative entities from annoying you. They may hang around the fringes of your sight as you move through the astral, but they are usually too cowardly to attack a confident astral traveler. Never consider yourself to be defenseless when in the astral. You can always defend yourself from undesirables.

Dangerous Entities and the Astral Police

There is a form of "astral police" who can be called upon for protection or to remove and restrain a threatening entity. These beings are easily identified by the brilliant white light which surrounds them. They will come instantly when you call. Some people mistakenly call these beings angels or guardian teachers, but they have a totally different function, type of aura, and vibration. They are police in the truest sense of the word, and are often just as overworked. It is their responsibility to patrol the astral levels, round up dangerous entities who escaped from the lower levels, and return them there. These astral police have the power to imprison these disturbed and disturbing entities, so that they can't harass humans, either on the physical or the astral.

Some humans help these dangerous entities "break jail," either deliberately or subconsciously, by constantly thinking about them and desiring or fearing their presence. Constant, intense fears of these entities will provide the energy needed for them to "escape" from the lower level. A human may have briefly met an entity and desires further contact, even though the astral being is a low-level spirit; or a human lover may have physically died and the mate left behind, totally disregarding what the person was really like when alive, wishes to continue the relationship.

When someone dies in the physical, their spiritual body enters the astral planes with all the prejudices, beliefs, desires, preconceived opinions, and behavior traits they had while alive. Naturally, this carries the spirit to the precise astral level where it will find like companions. If the spirit can find someone in the physical to whom it still has strong ties, it can use the emotions of that person or persons to make contact. Most deceased people are more concerned with attending spiritual classes, learning, and preparing for reincarnation than harassing a physical-bodied person and feeding off their energy.

The mother of a close friend was separated from her carousing, cheating, alcoholic husband for years, but refused to get a divorce because of her religion. He was a cruel, nasty-tempered, manipulating person who eventually died, but after his death, you would have thought he had been a saint to hear her talk. She created a set of memories which were all goodness, totally disregarding what the man was actually like. This gave her deceased husband what he needed to hook into her aura and travel around with her. Her health took a nose-dive; she had everything from sudden bypass surgery to hip replacement. Every time she visited her youngest son, he had to clean and seal the house after she left. The father created nightmares in the children, poltergeist activities, and general bad luck.

Never assume that all astral entities are concerned with your good or are capable of positive deeds and thoughts. What exists here on Earth exists also on the astral planes. The astral planes contain the scum of all earthly existence: the rapists, murderers, sex offenders, serial killers, thieves, incorrigible liars, and spouse abusers. Because these types of spirits are negative and corrupt in their thoughts and deeds, they are confined to the spiritual darkness of the lower astral levels. Occasionally, some of these "inmates" escape and accost astral travelers or humans in the physical body. However, there must be something within a personality to attract them.

When auras (in the physical or the astral) come in contact with each other, they immediately create and project hair-thin threads of auric energy. These threads connect the two auras, feeding emotions and data from one to the other. All communication between the connected individuals is accomplished through the subconscious mind and telepathy. Keep your intuitive senses alert while you are out on the astral planes. These senses will be your first warning signal if something is wrong or dangerous.

If you aren't certain about an astral entity, check on the emotions you are feeling from them. If the feeling is negative, remove yourself from their vicinity. Don't fall victim to feelings of fear, however, as this gives negative entities control over you. Be indignant that they should be bothering you at all. Order them to leave, call upon your teacher-guides, and return to your physical body if necessary. It is inevitable that at some time you will meet an astral being who makes you feel uncomfortable or afraid. When you are back in your body, analyze your emotions to see if you attracted such a being through your own personal problems. Be truthful, for if you lie to yourself, the person you hurt will be you! If you didn't attract them through some fault of your own, analyze what their presence may mean to you. If you would have been attracted to this type of person in the past, your teachers may have been testing you to see if your spiritual and emotional changes are firmly set.

After being in close proximity to such an astral being, or being harassed or attacked by one, you should take the time to cleanse and rebalance your chakras and clean your aura. If you are experiencing feelings of guilt or negativity, perform these personal rituals before you even attempt to astral travel. In fact, it will be a good idea if you make these part of your daily routine. This procedure is presented in detail in Chapter Five.

Be on guard against created thoughtforms sent to you by someone who has sexual fantasies about you. This is a rare occurrence, but it can happen. These thoughtforms are just as aggressive as low astral entities, and they can be ejected in the same way. Immediately call for your teachers, astral lover, and the astral police to remove these thoughtforms, and either imprison them or return them to the sender. Then take precautions, by ritual if necessary, so they can no longer invade your environment or aura. You may or may not know the person who created these sexual fantasy thoughtforms. People who create them usually don't do it consciously, but that doesn't make them any less annoying or threatening. If the person in question expends constant emotion and thought on

these fantasies, the resulting thoughtforms can be quite powerful in the astral.

Ghosts in the Astral

Part of the astral world contains what we call ghosts. More
advanced souls exist in astral surroundings they create to
reflect their personal ideas of an afterlife. These are the
benign souls of friends and family who still care deeply about
us, who give us advice in dreams, who visit during meditation. These spirits sometimes appear, visibly or invisibly,
around people and places where they were once happy, and of
which they have fond memories. They are never negative.

The negative, malicious ghosts belong on the lower astral
levels; however, their fierce desire for a place or person has
allowed them to escape. The low-level ghosts can be bound
to a place by strong, usually negative, emotions. This may
have occurred at the time of their death, when an emotion
such as hatred or deep fear was uppermost in their mind.
These ghosts can be troublesome, creating atmospheres of
great uneasiness and fear, nightmares for people who try to
live in "their" house, and influencing the minds of depressed
or addicted persons.

More advanced ghosts are not bound to a specific place,
but come and go as they will. These spirits visit people and
places which have meaning and fond memories for them. If
they are pleased with the people who move into "their"
home, these spirits create an atmosphere of happiness and
good luck. Even if they are displeased, they seldom, if ever,
cause any trouble. They attempt to help loved ones who are
still in the physical.

Contacting the "Terror"

Sooner or later, depending upon your spiritual progress, you will meet a special astral creature which you yourself created. This is and is not a thoughtform, such as I have talked about before. Everyone has one of these creatures; there are no exceptions. In the occult field this frightening, but benevolent, being is called "The Terror of the Threshold." Contacting the "Terror" can be especially difficult, because this entity reflects in its appearance all of your deepest fears, and it will appear in the form which frightens you most. You have to pass the test of overcoming your fears before you can further your spiritual growth, advance in spiritual knowledge and learn some of the ancient mystical secrets.

Some travelers are never able to come to terms with this entity. These people are unable or unwilling to overcome the fears and lies which they have been fed—and which they believe—about the astral and magick. No one else can help you pass the Terror of the Threshold. Instead you must accept personal responsibility, and do what is necessary. You are responsible for the positive and negative ideas and information in your mind. When you can face this guardian in the proper manner, it will transform into a totally different creature. If it doesn't transform, you can be certain that you have some deeply buried fears and preconceptions to weed out.

The Terror has another duty: it guards your physical body from being disturbed or harassed by astral entities, and keeps such beings from challenging your astral body when you return to the physical. The Terror is a powerful ally for all astral travelers who have successfully met, talked with, and passed the Terror of the Threshold.

The Dangers of Negative Entities

It is always wise to call upon your teacher-guides or astral lover before embarking on any astral journey. These benevolent beings will act as guides to the proper place, protectors from any predatory astral entities, and consultants to help you understand what you see. Your regular teachers have chosen to see to your basic education during your physical lifetime; however, there are many other wise teachers, priestesses and priests, and highly advanced spiritual beings in the astral who can help you to find information you are seeking, contact other spirits, and discover your true astral lover.

When you reach a certain stage of your development, your teachers will often arrange or allow you to stumble upon a negatively slanted entity or experience in the astral to teach you to be cautious and aware at all times. They won't let you come to any harm, but they may let you experience some pretty frightening things before rescuing you. I guarantee that an experience or two of this nature will cure you of ever wanting to dabble in negative astral energies, or mess around with lower-level beings.

Whenever you go out onto the astral planes, whether it is by deliberate methods or while asleep, you take with you all the emotions—positive and negative—which are clinging to your life and your emotional body. You take responsibility for where you go on the astral and what you see there by truthfully acknowledging and dealing with your emotional problems. This often involves a lot of painful self-examination and self-discipline, but the benefits are well worth the trouble. Living in a state of denial merely denies you spiritual growth.

Low-level negative entities and unpleasant astral experiences can also be attracted to you by negative physical relationships. If you are involved in a relationship which degrades you or is morally wrong, you can expect to eventually be faced with negative astral beings. Alcoholics, drug addicts, and constantly negative people drag undesirable entities around with them all the time. If you think this is impossible, spend about five minutes in a crowded bar full of drunks. If you are psychic, you will be able to see the negative entities riding around on people. Even if you are not psychic, the aura of such a place and the people there will send you running for a quick shower.

Keep your physical and astral morals high to draw to yourself entities or thoughtforms of desirable types and levels. This is especially true in terms of astral lovers and astral lovemaking. If you are unethical in your astral lovemaking excursions, or are into this kind of astral experience just for the thrills, I won't tell you that you will immediately be blasted for your "sin"; but you can be sure that at some time you will attract a really nasty low-level entity who will hook into your vibrations and plague you on both the physical and astral planes. Since like attracts like in vibrations, there will be no way you can avoid this kind of self-retribution.

If you have been told, or talked yourself into believing, that no physical person can affect you through their magickal efforts or negative thoughts, then you had better prepare yourself for problems. I'm not talking about Satanism, which is a religion perverted from Christianity; dark magick and ill-wishing have nothing to do with religion. Any person can wish you ill, and any magician who is jealous, feels threatened, or thinks you are impeding their progress in some way can, and might, cast a spell against you.

Constantly dwelling on thoughts of revenge or harm to another is also a form of mental magick. Since thoughts are things and have power, they may create an astral being which will harass you on your astral travels. The ill-wishing person's distance from you makes no difference, since the desired effect is shaped on the astral. Some magicians do not need a piece of your clothing, a lock of hair, or even a letter handwritten by you to zero in on your vibrations and cause problems. Knowing that such negative magicians and their thoughtforms exist doesn't mean you have to have a paranoid attitude toward astral travel; all you need to do is use common sense, take sensible precautions, and stay alert.

Most magicians and astral travelers are not in much danger from their fellow humans. The greatest dangers come from negative astral entities who resent your spiritual and astral progress. Everyone who travels on the astral planes learns that there are undesirable, often dangerous, entities living there. Sometimes we are subjected to these entities through the habits of someone close to us, and not by our own habits or actions. Deliberately consorting with or having sexual contact with low-level or negative astral entities is certain to contaminate you with what I call "psychic lice," or "psychic venereal disease." These lice hook into your aura and infect it. They subtly change your auric vibrations so that you become a magnet for every negative, wandering thoughtform, regardless of how small. These astral lice, unless removed and your attitude changed, will eventually cause a breakdown in your auric shield, opening you to actual physical disease, emotional trauma, and a decline in everything from prosperity to good luck. Once in your aura, these astral microbes will continue to grow, feeding off your auric energy, and attracting negatives until you get rid of them.

Like humans, astral entities have auras, and all auras contain energy particles which can transfer from one aura to another. You should strive to attract positive energy particles to your aura. "Lying down with dogs and getting up with fleas" applies as much to the astral as it does to Earth. Hanging around on either the astral or physical with entities who aren't of a high quality will contaminate your aura with negative energy particles, and you will have to work very hard to get rid of these "fleas" and their influences.

There are also certain deceased astral beings who gain strength at the expense of physical humans. Such entities are called "psychic vampires," and attach auric threads to your aura and chakras to siphon off your energy. Most who do this, whether astral entity or astral traveler, are very sneaky; they usually don't confront you, but slip the auric threads in when they feel you are unaware of their presence. Unfortunately, there are also human psychic vampires who feed off the energy of friends and acquaintances; but most of them would not believe you if you told them what they were doing. These are friends who are always having a bad time with life, and who seldom take positive action or personal responsibility to make it better. They visit you feeling depressed and terrible; and by the time they leave, they feel wonderful, but you feel depressed and terrible. This auric attachment can also take place through phone calls with certain determined physical "vampires."

If you return from an astral journey (or a visit with someone) and feel depleted, close your eyes for a few moments and visualize your aura. You will probably find a hair-thin auric thread coming from a distance, and connected to one of your light centers. Connection to the solar plexus, the area of emotions, is the most common. The only way to sever these auric threads, and keep them from reattaching themselves, is to visualize yourself with a white-hot sword in your hand. With one swift stroke of this imaged weapon, burn through the thread or threads. Then rebalance your chakras and clean your aura as described below.

Protection Ritual Against Negative Entities

This ritual is best done during the dark of the Moon or at New Moon, but can be performed any time there is a great need. You will require frankincense incense (sticks work fine); salt; a chalice or glass of water; a bell; white candle; and a piece of special jewelry which can be consecrated as a protection amulet. Before beginning, work out in your mind how you can move through every room, including the basement of your home, and end up near an outside door. If you have no one to help you, carry all your ritual tools on a tray with you from room to room.

Prepare for the ritual by taking a bath (not shower) with a little salt in the water. Wear your ritual robes, or at least a nice gown or robe, and prepare your altar. (This can be as simple as a TV tray if you don't have a regular altar.) Set the white candle in the center toward the back of the altar, and the salt on a small dish in front of it alongside the water. Light the incense and carry it around the room clockwise, beginning at one side of the door and ending at the other side. Say:

> *This room is purified on all levels. Only those entities of pure heart and high spiritual purpose may enter here.*

Return the incense to the altar and light the white candle and say:

> *Bright as the spiritual protective light around me, this candle is a beacon to all those on spirit side who would help me with this ritual.*

Add a small amount of salt to the chalice of water and swirl it clockwise to mix. Take the piece of jewelry and pass it carefully through the incense smoke and above the candle flame, then sprinkle it lightly with the water, and say:

> *This magickal blessed amulet will warn me of*
> *any psychic attack and protect me from all those*
> *who wish me ill.*

Take the bell in your power hand and, moving clockwise, circle the room, ringing the bell. Always start your ritual movements at one side of an exit door and end at the other side. When you return to your position at the altar, set aside the bell. Take the chalice and, moving around the room clockwise, anoint the sides of every window and mirror in the room. Place the incense, water chalice, and bell on your tray. Go entirely through every room in your house, including the basement, first with the incense, then the ringing bell, followed by the water anointing. When you have cleansed every room, you should find yourself near an outside door. Set aside your tray, open the door, and order all negative entities to leave at once. It helps to ring the bell as they leave. Negative entities don't like the sound of bells, gongs, tambourines, or cymbals.

Return to your altar with your tray. Raise your arms in greeting to your spiritual teachers and guardians. Say:

> *Fill this home with goodness, spiritual light,*
> *and all other positive things. I thank you for*
> *your aid and ask for your continued blessings.*

Extinguish the candle and save it in case you need to do another cleansing ritual. Let the incense burn out. Clean your chalice of water and put everything away.

Any time you cleanse a place or a person, including yourself, you need to fill the void with high spiritual vibrations afterwards. If you don't, every negative thing you cast out will return. It is a natural law that voids should be filled; it's up to you to see that the void is filled with something much better than what you had to begin with.

Part of this cleansing should include a physical cleaning. Clutter is one thing; we all live in one stage or another of clutter (I always have so many projects going that for years I've told people I decorate in Early Clutter), but dirtiness as the result of laziness is inexcusable and detrimental to your spiritual well-being. It also draws and harbors negative entities. This also applies to basements, garages, and attics which are total chaos because no one wants to spend the time cleaning them. After you have cleaned and cleansed your personal physical living space, you need to go into meditation to cleanse and fortify the astral space around you.

Protection Meditation

Prepare yourself in a cleansing bath with a little salt added to the water. Set up your meditation space with special care. Make certain it is cleaned, and carry frankincense incense around the room. Since smoking incense in an enclosed space can make you very uncomfortable, it might be a good idea to let it burn out in another room while you are meditating.

Prepare yourself for the meditation as usual: silent phone, pets out of the room, do-not-disturb sign on the door, and soft non-vocal music to cover small noises. Then see yourself by the well where you can dump all the negative things and people who are causing you distress. Surround yourself mentally with the white light. Spend as much time as necessary relaxing your body.

When you are ready, move out onto the astral planes, going directly to your specially created place. Enter your sacred space or temple and sit before the altar. Call upon the Goddess/God in your own words, telling Her/Him about the problems you are having with psychic harassment or attack. As you sit in contemplation, you become aware that a number of astral beings are entering the temple. These are powerful, positive entities. They form a circle around the entire temple space with you in the center. You ask:

Why is this happening?

These teachers, guides, magicians, and protectors will tell you exactly why, so listen closely. Be very careful that you are actually hearing their words, not what you want to hear. At least some of the reasons given will have been caused by you. If you have had any negative astral entities attached to your aura or astral body, you may well see them fleeing the rising tide of positive vibrations bombarding you from all sides. You ask:

What can I do to stop this?

Again these powerful beings will supply answers. They may immediately work to cleanse your aura and astral body. Whatever they do, they will also tell you what you yourself should be doing to avoid this problem in the future. When these beings are finished, they will again move into the great circle, chanting and singing. The words may make no sense to you, since the language used is a tongue known only to the high-level beings of the astral plane. The temple becomes filled with blazing white light and great energy. As the chanting stops, you hear the temple ring like a great bell.

This group of powerful entities now takes you into the astral area around your physical home. They encircle the dwelling place as they did the temple, chanting and singing, until the vibrations of your home begin to pulsate with light and give off a delicate sound like wind chimes. Your astral helpers fade away, leaving you to return to your temple or go back into your physical body.

If it seems that I have driven home the dangers of the astral planes, you are correct. It is better to know of all the dangers, even if you never meet them, than to be totally unprepared. There are, however, many wonderful, benign, exciting beings on the astral planes who will be happy to interact with you in a positive manner. Nature spirits, mythical creatures, deities, and the souls of animals dwell on certain areas of the five intermediate levels. Very elemental and simple Nature spirits are mostly on the second astral level, while the souls of animals, depending upon their development, are found on any of the middle areas. Astral animal familiars are favorite companions of shamans and witches. They can be very helpful in the practice of magick and the development of psychic senses. If you form a deep friendship with a particular familiar, it will also act as an additional guardian for both your physical life and astral excursions. Familiars are also a lot of fun.

Faeries and Elves

Humans have a long history of encountering faeries and elves. From very early times, there are traditions of humans willingly or unwillingly entering Faeryland, where time has no meaning.

Lady Wilde of Ireland cites examples of young men in particular being lured away by the song and music of the faeries. The music of many dance tunes, such as the "Faery Dance" of Scotland, and the "Londonderry Air" of Ireland, are said to have been memorized by fiddlers and pipers from faery music they encountered. The music of Londonderry Air is so faery-like that human words never quite seem to fit. The famous piper of the Mac Crimmon family is said to have learned his skill from a faery man when he was a boy.

Faeryland itself is described over and over as a place of endless delight and great beauty. Many artistic, open-minded people visited Faeryland and returned to cautiously express their experiences in literature, music, and art. William Butler Yeats (1865-1939), although he was known as a practical person, firmly believed in faeries. Some of his beautiful, haunting poetry carries embedded within it the sounds of wistful faery music. Aubrey Beardsley's artwork expresses both the sensuality and the fantasy of the faery world.

Probably the best-known mortal inhabitant of Faeryland (some versions say Elfland) is Thomas the Rhymer, who lived in Scotland in the thirteenth century. In documents of his time, he is called Thomas Rymour de Ercildoune. The Queen of Elfland fell in love with Thomas, taking him to her palace, and keeping him there for seven years. At the end of that time, she returned him to Earth with the gift of truth-telling. He became famous throughout Scotland for his prophecies. In later life, as Thomas gave a feast one night, a hind and a doe appeared at his castle. He followed them into the woods and never returned. No body was ever discovered (a total contrast to Robert Kirk who was declared taken by faeries but whose body was buried). Visitors to Faeryland tell of seeing Thomas the Rhymer there. The tree where Thomas is said to have met the Faery Queen is still pointed out to visitors. (A supposedly "traditional" part of this story says the Queen returned Thomas to Earth to avoid sacrificing him to the devil; but this is obviously an insert by some Christian writer.)

Women were also said to be taken by the faeries. Some went as nursing mothers to faery babies; others were called to help with a faery birth. A few were chosen to be faery brides. A faery bride story is that of Sir Launfal, told in a medieval romance. It appears that the faeries need to infuse faery blood with human blood and vigor at intervals. Children born to mortal men and women who have taken faery lovers, primarily stayed in Faeryland. A few women, as mentioned in Robert Kirk's book, bore physical children to faery lovers upon their return to the human world. All the stories of female faeries marrying mortal men are stories of captured brides. The only exception to this were the Gwrachs of Wales, who could be wooed and won by mortal men.

There are many stories of rescues or attempted rescues of mortal women. The Irish have the legend of Midhir and Etain, an epic about the rescue of a mortal woman from Faeryland. Several stories tell of unwilling captives in Faeryland who are befriended and helped to escape by another mortal who has chosen to stay there. In the Irish tales this is often a red-haired man.

Faeries do not like humans prying into their affairs or spying upon them. Certain kinds of faeries never reveal their names to mortals; yet at the same time, humans and their lives seem to be of great importance to faeries and elves.

The shaman, magicians, and astral travelers will find themselves in contact many times with the faery folk. Although many anthropologists consider faeries to be no more than ancient deities, common sense says that this is not true. The Celts, for instance, were quite clear in their writings and legends that the deities were gods and goddesses, while the Good Folk were a separate race of supernatural beings.

Most faeries and elves have the ability to change their size and appearance at will; but the very tiny faeries do not seem to have this ability. Among the human-sized faeries are the White Ladies, Fays, and Faery Knights. Their choice of clothing can range from modern fashions to archaic. Particularly in Celtic countries, the favorite color of faeries is said to be green followed by red. Elves seem to prefer green and brown; however, they do not confine themselves to these colors, but wear whatever pleases them. Whether large or small, faeries and elves like dancing, music, hunting, processional rides, hurling contests, chess, and occasionally war. Their dancing is primarily circular in nature, and is the most frequent activity mentioned in connection with faeries. If they have no companions, they will leap and dance alone. Faeries hunt faery deer with their hounds (white with red ears) but don't kill them.

Elves came originally from Scandinavia, but as with a great many faeries or other spirits, traveled along with emigrants to new countries. Legend says there are two classes of elves: the light elves and the dark elves. In Scotland human-sized, supernatural beings were called elves, while the diminutive ones were known as faeries. Faeryland was known as Elfame. Elves do not like to be called faeries, nor faeries elves, as faeries are a distinct class of beings from elves. They will also be among the first to tell you that they are not related to deities. All types of Nature spirits and supernatural beings have their own cultures and histories, and come in more than one size and coloring. If you should happen to seek your astral lover, or even guidance and help, from among these beings, learn their differences, customs, and appearances to avoid unintentional insult.

In Manx, the faery folk are sometimes called *ferish*, but mostly "The Little People," (Mooinjer veggey) or "Little

Boys" (Guillyn veggey). In Ireland and Wales, they were commonly called the "Good Folk," the "Wee Folk," the "Good Neighbors," or other positive names to avoid antagonizing them. One of the earlier names for faeries was *fays*. Today the term, faery, has come to cover Anglo-Saxon and Nordic elves, the Daoine Sidhe of the Highlands, the Tuatha De Danann of Ireland, the Tylwyth Teg of Wales, the Seelie and Unseelie Courts, brownies, and many more. Faeries can be malicious or helpful, often depending upon previous experiences with astral-traveling humans. They are leery about first contacts; so be patient upon meeting them. Elves are not faeries, any more than faeries are brownies or wood nymphs. Unfortunately, elves have been included as part of the faery culture for so long, that people have forgotten many of their characteristics and habits.

The Celts believed that the faery folk were in constant contact with future possibilities. If a person attracted and worked with a Co-walker (or faery companion) that person could become a seer or predictor, who sees into the future. Often these seers used the technique of looking through a knothole or a ring in order to get a better view of the astral world (Otherworlds), and their faery companions. The same effect can be produced by forming a small tunnel with the slightly clenched fingers of your hand. As you look through this tunnel, you will be able to see pictures against the darkened area of the hand. In records dating from Christian times, the Scottish seers spoke of a terrifying sight when first the Second Sight is used: astral entities seem to rush toward the seer from all directions. This seems logical, since astral entities of all types want to be recognized. When they discover someone who has learned how to see or travel into the astral, these Otherworld beings rush from all directions for recognition, another reason for keeping your morals high and seeking higher planes. Being descended upon by crowds of astral beings can be a little overwhelming, but just stand your ground, feel confident about your abilities, and send out a mental S.O.S. to your teacher or astral lover if you feel you need help. Most higher astral entities will back off as soon as they realize you know what you are doing.

The Celts also taught that seers who had positive thoughts and actions attracted positive Otherworld companions, while those harboring negative thoughts and deeds drew only negative beings. The Celts said that if a person did something negative, the positive Co-walker would leave. (We might call this Co-walker a faery-elfin teacher-guide.) Since you attract entities with vibrations similar to your own, it is logical that a higher teacher would leave if your vibrational rate dropped into the negative range.

The Faery Rade is often mentioned in writings and legends. This Rade was really a processional ride on horses, a creature valued by faeries and elves. However, the wild faery horses, sometimes with fiery eyes, were known for their fierceness, a trait soon experienced by would-be human thieves. Faery cattle were less wild, often mingling with the cattle of humans. They ordinarily came and went in herds, except for the solitary and beneficent cows like the Dun Cow of Kirkham. Farmers were overjoyed when their cattle were visited by elf-bulls; the offspring resulting from the breeding between the elf-bull and mortal cattle were superior in every way.

In nearly every country which has faeries and elves (and almost every country in the world does) traditions say that there are certain specific hours when faeries can be seen by the physical eyes. Usually this sighting is enhanced by looking through a naturally holed stone, using a four-leafed clover, or sighting a faery knowe (hill or mound) or faery ring in the grass through a knothole or your semi-clenched fist. The hours when faeries traditionally are seen are twilight, noon, midnight, and the hour before sunrise. As long as you keep a faery in sight, it cannot escape; but if you so much as blink an eye, it vanishes.

Some astral inhabitants are known as elemental spirits, the spirits who represent and work with the Elements of Earth, Air, Fire, and Water. Unless you are an accomplished magician, it isn't wise to call up or entice the presence of elemental spirits; they can be very unpredictable, difficult to handle, and sometimes downright dangerous. Other inhabitants of the astral planes are creatures such as Pan, fauns, wood and water nymphs, mermaids and mer-men, angels, and every other creature written about in ancient legends.

Besides giving you a very simplistic overview of the astral planes and the beings who dwell there, all this information will help you to find your astral lover. I imagine that when you first read the term "astral lover" you had a human-like image in your mind. It is true that many, if not most, astral lovers were human at one time in their existence; however, you are not confined to human-spirit lovers. Once comfortable with such an astral lover, you may be approached by an elf or faery, nymph or even the god Pan. You may decide to experience an Otherworld lover who never had a human life.

Unlike many of the stories about faery lovers, one does not have to live in Faeryland to experience a faery or elfin lover. During the English Civil War, there lived a young girl named Anne Jefferies in St. Teath in Cornwall. In 1645, she became unconscious for a period of time. When she recovered, she possessed prophetic powers. It was some time before she revealed that she had been in Faeryland, and had a faery lover in the fullest sense of the word. The difference between Anne's lover and other faery lovers was that he kept the relationship going while she was in the physical body and totally conscious of what was happening. Finally, under constant pressure and persecution from the Church, and the scandalized church-going men, Anne Jefferies broke off the relationship. Although she seldom talked about her experiences, she never changed her story.

On very rare occasions, the Goddess as the Earth Mother and the God as the Lord of the Forests and Animals may present themselves in a ritualistic manner which will include a type of sex magick. This is highly spiritual and far above any other kind of astral love. The Goddess may present Herself to women, the God to men, as well as to the opposite sex.

Meditation: Meeting Benevolent Non-Human Entities

Begin by entering your astral meditation as usual, calling up the white light and dumping your negatives. Relax your body and then move out onto the astral planes to your special place. See yourself standing near the bottom of a great hill, its rounded sides covered with green grass, wild roses, old oaks, foxgloves, and ferns. Look very intently at the hill before you and see the faint outline of a great double-door hidden in the grass. The distant sound of beautiful music seems to be coming from inside the hill itself. As you reach out to push against the misty gates, a swarm of tiny brightly-colored faeries flies around you. They too push against the gates, and the great doors swing silently open. The tiny faeries fly ahead into the dark interior, beckoning and calling to you. You follow them.

As you hurry down the passageway, the gates close behind you. Following the glowing lights of the little faeries, you step out of the tunnel to find yourself in a wondrous place. All around you is a world of fantastic beauty, brilliant colors, and wonderful beings. The enticing music still floats through the air, as your tiny faery friends disappear into the great grassy meadow starred with flowers and surrounded by a dense forest. Through the meadow flows a bubbling stream edged with cattails, rushes, and water flowers. In the center of the meadow is a great stone-walled castle, pennants flying in the breeze. You follow the narrow path through the meadow and across the stream by an arched bridge, until you stand before the open gates of the castle itself.

Two big, white dogs with red ears rush out to greet you, leaping around you, yipping in happiness. Sedately strolling after them are several cats. They weave around your legs, purring and enticing you to follow them inside. A tall, handsome man walks through the gates. He is dressed in tight green trousers and jerkin, brown boots, a brown cap with a white feather on his head, and a smile curving his mouth. From his belt hang a sword and jeweled dagger. His golden-brown hair curls about his slightly pointed ears. With him is a woman wearing a long gown of blue satin and a glowing pendant on her breast. Her black hair ripples down her back, nearly reaching her knees.

"Welcome," the man says as he takes your hands and looks deep into your eyes. "Welcome to our land, human traveler."

"Enter and join our feasting," the woman smiles as she takes your arm in hers and walks through the gates into the castle yard.

These Otherworld beings take you into the great banquet hall, where hundreds of other faeries and elves sit at long tables. Musicians are playing pipes, harps, drums, and lutes for the gathering. The tables are full of wonderful things to eat and drink. Silver goblets, golden plates, and crystal bowls of fruit decorate each place. They escort you to an empty seat, then return to their high-backed chairs at the end of the hall. You look around at the hosts of faeries and elves, noting their appearance and clothing. You realize that all of the beings present are human-sized. Your table companions smile and talk with you, answering any questions you pose. As you listen and watch, you become aware of the subtle differences between elves and faeries.

You taste the food and drink, experiencing wonderful flavors you never thought possible. When the meal is finished, everyone leaves the banquet hall and goes into an adjoining room which is even bigger. There are elaborate chairs and benches around the edges of the room, and small tables with goblets and pitchers near each cluster of seats. The musicians mount a raised platform at one end of the room, and begin to play. The Otherworld Folk choose partners for the dance. You watch as they circle and twirl around the polished floor.

A faery being comes to your side, pulling you gently onto the dance floor. You find yourself in his or her arms, caught up in the music, and enjoying yourself. You change dancing partners from time to time, eventually coming back to your original partner. Your faery partner escorts you to a chair to rest, and pours out a goblet of sparkling drink for you. As you sit there together, the two of you talk about Faeryland, its inhabitants, and its customs. You learn many exciting things you never knew before.

When you are ready to return to your world, your faery companion walks with you, back across the meadow to the tunnel leading to the great gates in the hill. As you stand near the open gates, you may or may not exchange a kiss; this is up to you. Your Otherworld companion tells you that you can return any time you wish, and he or she will be waiting. As you step through the gates, you feel yourself sliding through astral space back into your physical body.

After several meetings with your faery/elfin companion, you may decide to take him or her as an astral lover, as well as having an astral human lover from your past. It is rare that either will be jealous of the other. Consider this faery/elfin relationship carefully, for these Otherworld beings are even more aggressive about making you face responsibility. They absolutely will not tolerate lying, either to others or to yourself.

If you use your astral love relationship in a productive, positive manner, your entire life, on all its levels, will strengthen and benefit. This lover, or lovers, will remain with you as long as you wish to continue the relationship.

Five

❧

Friendship vs. Courtship

Obviously you will not be considering friendships or astral love with all of the entities you meet on the astral; no more than you would every person you meet in the physical. Excluding the slimy low-level ones, you will have a broad selection of potential astral friends and lovers, although the vast majority of these beings will be only acquaintances, occasionally-seen friends, teachers, advisors, or mentors.

I strongly suggest that you take your time choosing an astral lover. Start by establishing friendships with as many astral beings as possible. To get friends, one must be friendly. Remember to be polite, don't exaggerate your accomplishments and importance, and be sincere in learning as much as you can from astral teachers. If you exaggerate or lie about yourself, they will know instantly; the word will quickly get around, and you will find yourself shunned by the very astral beings who could be of the most help to you.

Your Teacher-Guides

Some of the first helpful astral entities you will probably meet are your own special teacher-guides. Forget about "bands" and all the other buzz words, and the false idea that more teachers means a higher spiritual human. It is quality, not quantity, that counts. The number of teachers around a person varies constantly, depending upon what you are currently studying, practicing, or doing. Some come to help you for a short time, while you are learning a new subject, then move on to let others take their place. A few remain with you for all or most of an Earth lifetime, provided, of course, that you do not slip backwards. As you evolve, you gain more advanced teachers who can impart higher levels of learning on specific areas of study or on completely new areas of knowledge. If you lose ground spiritually and morally and begin to devolve, higher teachers will leave and their place be taken by entities of a lower caliber.

These teacher-guides are simply beings who are in the astral at the present time and have chosen to help and instruct you. You may have heard the idea of Native American guides being considered the mark of the "elite" in spiritualism. This idea comes from the early days of spiritualism, but is not necessarily correct. Teacher-guides come from various nationalities, cultures, time periods, and abilities. They may include some of your own ancestors (recently deceased or out of the far past). Some of these teachers may well have remained on the astral for centuries, growing, learning, and passing on knowledge by helping humans still in earthly life.

Teachers come in all degrees of advancement, knowledge, morals, and interests. Their personalities basically remain the same as when they inhabited a physical body. Their sense of humor may range from very dry to outright prankster; a few seem to have no sense of humor at all, and are always extremely serious. Some teachers are tolerant of mistakes, while others are outspoken and even caustic with their remarks on your behavior. There are large numbers of astral teachers who specialize in certain areas of knowledge. To be coached by one of these is like taking a class from a teacher with a Master's degree in a certain subject; you had best listen closely and be polite. A great many of them are from ancient civilizations and times, some of whose history is now lost to us. By actively seeking out these teachers of very ancient history, you can learn old techniques of spirituality and the psychic which have been forgotten on this plane of existence. They will expect you to be sincere, work hard, and keep a regular class schedule.

There are also teachers who can instruct you in art, music, ancient ceremonies, mystic secrets—any subject you can imagine. If you desire to expand your knowledge in a specialized area, these are the astral teachers to seek out. If you are not meant to study a particular subject, these teachers will not hesitate to tell you so and will direct you to a teacher and subject which will benefit you. If you learn that you knew and practiced a certain art in past lives, do not assume that you will quickly and easily regain such knowledge this time. You knew how to walk in every lifetime you have lived, but you had to relearn the hard way every time you were reborn.

There are special counselors who work with the Akashic records, the repository of information about every life of every person ever incarnated in a physical body. These counselors can help you look at your past lives, analyze what now affects you, and determine how you can make changes to avoid further painful experiences. Karma is both positive and negative; it is put into action by both the good and bad actions and decisions you made in the past, and the ones you are making now. Don't fall for the lie that karma is involved only with the negative things that happen to you; it isn't that simple.

Beginners look into the Akashic records out of curiosity, and with the hope that they were important, powerful, or famous. This is a normal reaction, but it is very unlikely that you were a famous historical figure. The world is primarily run by the actions and reactions of the everyday person whose main concern is getting food on the table. Searching through your Akashic records soon takes on another perspective if you are serious about your spiritual growth: You begin to see relationship patterns, behavior traits, buried talents, even physical problems. The thread of these patterns may run through several lives, right down to the present one.

If you are sincere in your desire for spiritual enlightenment, an Akashic counselor will reveal to you the connections between past and present relationships, one of the biggest stumbling-blocks or one of the greatest aids in human advancement. This can be a great eye-opener, especially if you are currently uncertain about continuing or ending a friendship or relationship. Just because you loved or lived with someone in another life does not make them your ideal mate or friend this time. Look carefully for buried emotions in those past lives which you might have missed at the time: jealousy, a need to control, intimidation, revenge, possessiveness, manipulation. One of the biggest negatives you can create is to cause someone to feel guilty about leaving a relationship. If you find such a thread, don't accept that it occurred only in one lifetime. Follow it back to as close to the beginning of the problem as you can get. You may or may not have initiated the trouble, but you need not continue it.

There is an old saying about karma: Never teach karma to anyone not willing and prepared to overcome it. The only reason to look through your Akashic records is to improve yourself. You are responsible for your reactions, your attitudes, your desires, your morals, your spiritual goals. Sometimes we don't know when to stop punishing ourselves for past mistakes. If an incident was accompanied by intense, subconscious, emotional feelings of regret, pain, hatred, or guilt, we tend to keep attracting events which will punish us for mistakes we made a lifetime, or many lifetimes, ago. If we can honestly say that we learned the lesson, we can disconnect from that emotionally generated punishment; however, you can't lie, either to yourself or to the Akashic counselors. If you didn't really learn the lesson, nothing you say or do will deflect the reaction you set in motion.

Too many people learn only limited knowledge about karma and think they understand it. One of the biggest fallacies about karma is that if someone hurt you in some way, that person will have to right the wrong directly to you in some future life. If you believe this, then that person will certainly reappear in one of your lives; however, there is no guarantee that he or she will right the wrong. Knowing human nature, the wrongdoer will probably do it to you again. Personally, I would rather such a person should attempt to balance the scales in another way, having nothing to do with me. Usually by the time I am consciously aware of the intrinsic negativity of such a person, he or she has already had several lifetimes to compound the original misdeed. In other words, there were plenty of opportunities to change, but he or she chose to continue his or her negative actions. I take what precautions I can to permanently sever any subconscious ties, and not to feel guilty about it.

Evaluating a Potential Lover

Always check out astral lovers (or any astral beings) before
becoming involved in any way. Your first impressions (or intuitive feelings) can be invaluable in this process. Be very aware
of their actions and the way they approach you. Also listen
carefully to exactly what is said and how it is worded. Are the
astral beings quick to suggest that you trust them? That you
take their every word as absolute truth without question? Do
they order you to make drastic changes in your life? Do they
subtly suggest immoral activities? Have you caught them in an
outright lie? After contact with these entities, do you feel like
you need a physical and spiritual bath? These are all warning
signs of low-level or negative astral beings. One easy, quick
method to weed out undesirable astral beings is to remember
to surround yourself with brilliant white light before you go
out onto the astral planes. This light will cause immediate discomfort and often pain to low-level entities, regardless of how
nice they represent themselves to be.

Low-level entities will be attracted to you particularly if
you are engaged in the use of drugs, alcohol, or in indiscrim-
inate sexual activity; or if you have been through a very emo-
tionally-draining time, are depressed, or have a low opinion
of yourself. They will also approach you if you are conceited
and think you can handle anything. If you fall into this last
category, you can become prey for some of the stronger and
more dangerous low-level entities. This type of entity likes to
play games with ego-centered humans, stringing them along
until they are in over their heads, then bringing everything
crashing down in a really horrible way.

If you meet someone who says they were an acquaintance
or lover in past lives, it is a good idea to look at your Akashic
records with an open mind before becoming too involved.

The two of you might have had bad experiences together. If this is the case, let the entity in question rebalance his or her karma in another way which excludes you. You may discover that the relationship was a happy one, but that you have changed greatly since then, and that you no longer have much in common. In your present life, have you reconnected with old friends you haven't seen for years only to find that the friendship can no longer be continued? People can change greatly, even within a single lifetime. A relationship which worked in one lifetime may not be desirable now.

Before you decide upon calling to an old acquaintance or lover, look at yourself in other lives compared to the way you are now. How have you changed? How have your choices of companions, friends, and lovers changed? If you take the time to look closer at what the other "yous" were like, you will save yourself a lot of grief when choosing astral lovers.

Sometimes we think someone new and unknown will be better. Often this is because we are undecided about ourselves and our desires, or simply like the idea of a new, unknown lover. If you are the undecided type, then you are going through friends and lovers like mad in your physical life, taking and never giving in relationships, always retreating when things get serious or you are asked to give of yourself. If you have this flaw in your personality, you may well find it nearly impossible to see your own faults; however, it must be done if you are to grow and advance. If you don't or won't look at this negative, self-indulgent type of behavior, you will eventually find yourself slumming in the lower regions of the astral planes.

There is nothing wrong with wanting to explore totally new astral friendships and previously unknown astral lovers. As humans, we are always slowly adding and releasing friends and acquaintances. As it is in this life, so it has been through many lives. This adding and releasing is a natural part of our personal growth process; but you don't discard *all* of the old in favor of all new. You should carefully scrutinize each relationship, weighing the positives and negatives. If you discover that someone is always taking and not sharing, or that your interests no longer walk the same paths, then you should begin to sever the friendship so that it dies on the vine.

New astral lovers can be exciting and stimulating to all areas of your life. Don't confine yourself to human-type astral beings. There are a number of other human-like entities who inhabit other planes of vibration, who have never been in a human physical body. Among these are faeries, elves, deities, demi-gods, and Nature-type spirits. Faeries and elves are some of the best astral lovers there are, and are imbued with their own special kind of powerful magick. Nature spirits include the naiads, nymphs, mer-people, Pan, the fauns and satyrs, among others.

The archetypal powers of the deities still exist on the astral planes, and they are true to their personalities related in old legends, so take care which ones you contact and why you contact them. The unnamed archetypal powers known as the Goddess and God are the most potent. One does not seek Them out; They come to you. The demi-gods were beings created from the astral union of a human and a deity. They are closer to humans than are deities, and more understanding of human needs. The sorcerer Merlin was such a being.

Always insist upon a period of friendship, possibly followed by a time of courtship, before becoming too deeply involved with any astral being. An entity who will not agree to a courtship period is not what you should be seeking. Work at developing the astral relationship, the same as you would an earthly one. Don't rush into anything, especially if you have a history of doing this in physical relationships.

Begin by setting very clear ground rules for both yourself and your lover. If you do this right at the start, any subtle manipulative deviations will be immediately apparent. Ask lots of questions. Were you together before? Where? Why? What was your relationship then? If this is a new relationship (which does sometimes occur), why does the astral being want to be with you? Any astral being who becomes annoyed or angry at these questions obviously is hiding something.

The courtship period should be a time of getting to know each other, to feel comfortable with each other's vibrations. When you are with this being, you should feel emotional comfort and satisfaction just from their presence, their touch, their words. Make the courtship last as long as you can. Avoid astral sex right away. Impatience for astral sex is a clue to a low-level entity or spirit. If and when you do decide to meld chakras with an astral being in lovemaking, avoid attachments to at least the lower three chakras. If you are reconnecting with a past lover who was with you through several lifetimes, you will probably meld chakras from the heart up. An old acquaintance or lover, who was also a teacher or mentor in some capacity, will meld first with the throat chakra. For very spiritual sexual-melding with high-level astral entities, the melding will be no lower than the brow chakra.

The Seven Light Centers

Since chakra melding takes the place of physical sex, you should be very aware of the condition of your own chakras before engaging in this activity. Having the light centers balanced and in good working order not only helps you to advance spiritually, but keeps your mental, emotional, and physical bodies in good health. Like any explorer into new territory, you want to go as prepared as possible.

Before beginning work on your own chakras, you should learn something about them and how their health or dis-ease affect all areas of your life, including your attitudes toward and choice of astral friends and lovers. Becoming aware of chakra functions, blockages, colors, and their meanings helps considerably during healing, whether of the self or another. Chakra colors often bleed over into the aura. They can be a clue to improvement needed in certain physical areas, or an indication of progress on a spiritual level. During meditation, the light centers are all open, however dim they may be. Disturbance or noise during this time causes an immediate shutdown of the chakras, an automatic precautionary measure taken by the astral body to avoid damage to the nervous system.

A working knowledge of the light centers, or chakras, is an important part of spiritual training. We are indebted to the Eastern philosophies for keeping alive many essential truths until Western civilizations were again ready to investigate this ancient wisdom. In the very distant past, humans, at various civilizations and centers around the world, were much more knowledgeable about the "total being" than we are today. Unfortunately, because of the rise and fall of both civilized learning centers and human spiritual growth, knowledge of the chakras has been buried under layers of wordy mysticism to preserve and protect it.

There are seven major light centers in the human body, which are lighted by a baby's first breath. Hindu philosophy lists other minor centers, such as in the palms of the hands and the soles of the feet, but these are not as important. It is possible that the seven major light centers of the astral body are connected in some way with the traditional seven levels of the astral planes.

The word chakra literally means "wheel of fire." They appear to the psychic as rapidly turning pools of light. In a highly spiritually developed person, the chakras will be large, very definite in color, and have a spinning movement to them. As a person advances in spiritual growth, these centers begin to open more and more, like a blossom opens petal by petal to the Sun. The more evolved a person is, the clearer and more perfect are the colors of the chakras, and the more definite their shape and movement.

Chakras are whirling intake centers, attached to the astral body. As generators and inlets they bring astral-cosmic energy into your astral body to keep its vitality (and that of your physical body) alive.* All chakras are radiated from the spinal region in the corresponding astral body, flaring toward the front of the astral body like great flowering trumpets. They are not actually *in* the physical body at all, although they directly affect the physical.

There is a correlation between the chakras running up the spinal area of the astral body and the World Tree which is such an important part of the shaman's tradition. The shaman climbs the Tree to reach the higher astral planes. Ceremonial magicians and Qabalists also have been going onto the astral plane for centuries using a method similar to the World Tree and meditation. Using the Tree of Life glyph, they work their way up through the *sephiroth* to the spiritual spheres. Both these traditional images represent a central support; both symbolize the human desire to rise above the physical realm into the greater spiritual worlds.

Do not, under any circumstances, try to awaken only certain light centers; this will cause greater imbalance than you

---

* For a more in-depth study of chakras, I recommend *Wheels of Life: A User's Guide to the Chakra System* by Anodea Judith. St. Paul: Llewellyn Publications, 1993.

already have. Also, do not attempt to deliberately raise the Kundalini, known as the "serpent fire" or "sacred cobra." Premature, deliberate raising of this "fire" without the spiritual enlightenment to control it is extremely dangerous. The rush upward would be exhilarating, but the uncontrolled force will eventually turn downward and inward. The user will become the victim. Persons who do this in black magick, negative metaphysics, or with drugs, for example, become obsessed with sexual aberrations and activities. Eventually there is a short circuit or burn-out, beginning in the astral body and spreading rapidly into the mental, emotional, and physical states. The end result will be mental imbalance and possibly insanity. There have been instances where a hard blow to the base of the spine, such as a fall, has triggered the Kundalini, but this is not a common occurrence. If spiritual development is cultivated, the Kundalini will begin rising through the chakras in a natural, controlled sequence, without your having to dwell upon it.

It is not uncommon for one or more chakras to be partially blocked or underdeveloped. This shows areas in the physical, mental, emotional, or spiritual attitudes which need to be carefully contemplated and corrected. Sometimes the reasons for this are obvious, but usually there are layers of causes from both the present life and past lives.

The Four Areas of Responsibility

Before you begin to work with the chakras, you need to clearly understand what your responsibilities are to yourself and to others. Each individual has four areas, or "houses," of responsibility which he or she must keep in balance in order to prevent blockage in the chakras. At birth, you gain self-awareness; this is your first responsibility. You need to fully know and love yourself. If you are harsh with yourself, demanding more than is necessary, or things which cannot be accomplished, you will be harsh and demanding with others.

The physical body, vehicle of the soul and mind, is the second responsibility. You must care for your physical body, keeping it as healthy as possible, and not going to extremes which would put it in danger. The environment needed to fulfill the needs and lessons of the present lifetime is the third responsibility. This includes family responsibilities which have been accepted as part of the learning process.

The fourth responsibility is the path of worship, and companions chosen for spiritual fellowship, however the individual defines and practices spirituality. A false spirituality is created when a person overbalances all other responsibilities with the fourth responsibility. True spiritual communion with the Ultimate Creative Force (by whatever name you call It) should be a constant activity, evident in the many little things of life, performed because it is something you enjoy and find fulfilling. It should never be a misguided rush of church participation, seeking to convince yourself and others that the amount of time and energy spent on church work equals the degree of your spirituality. Never take part in any spiritual group or church because you are trying to please others, or think it is the thing to do. Each person must find their own way to spirituality.

The true path to spiritual growth teaches moderation and balance in all areas of life. An out-of-balance astral traveler will attract astral entities who may not be positive and helpful. You certainly want to be in balance before you start seeking an astral lover. Keep these four houses of responsibility in mind as you study the chakras, for if they are out of balance, so will be the chakras. By going over the questions at the end of each chakra discussion, you will be better able to determine what is out of balance in your life and how to correct it.

Personal Examination

1. Examine your life as impersonally as possible in the areas of goals, relationships, feelings, and growth. List the negatives and positives for each. Keep this list and note all changes as you progress.

2. Practice visualizing the seven chakra colors during brief meditations. Always end these color meditations by surrounding yourself with white light. This has a balancing effect on the chakras and compensates for the overapplication of any one color.

3. Sit quietly with your eyes closed. Ask to be shown the colors most prominent in each of your light centers at the present time. Note the shade of color carefully. Make a list of these and refer back to them during your studies. Can you relate the off-shades of colors to the chakras which need work?

4. During your normal daily routine, check for prominent colors in the auras of people around you. Do these colors relate to areas of their lives which need work?

The Root Chakra

The first, and lowest, chakra is the root center, located at the base of the spine. It is associated with the organs of reproduction—the ovaries and testes—and should be a clear, healthy red. This is the traditional dwelling place of the Kundalini. The root chakra is associated with physical existence, reproduction, physical creativity, and survival. It is the center of wants and aspirations. Fears and lack of energy show up here. Its degree of development sets the pattern for success or failure, the establishment of goals, the search for achievement and unfoldment.

It also affects physical relationships, your ability to enjoy the sexual act, and whether or not you attract love.

On the astral level, the condition of this chakra determines the types of entities attracted to you. It also attracts or repels other forms of astral energy which could make you sick or open to disease. If the root chakra is unobstructed, the individual has a healthy attitude toward sexual and other physical sensations. A person involved in low moral sexual activities, addiction to alcohol or drugs, compulsive overeating, or refusal to accept responsibility for one's actions, has a blockage in this center. The blockage will be apparent in the small size, and the unhealthy, rather muddy or dark, coloring of the chakra. Low energy levels and diseases of the blood or reproductive organs will also cause a distortion of color in the root chakra.

People who have been deprived of security and love, especially during early childhood, often have a blockage in this center, unless they have worked their way through it. The same applies to people who have experienced sexual abuse. This may manifest itself in later life as diabetes or hypoglycemia (both blood diseases) or overweight. It is important to face these past events, because they have been allowed to influence your present life. However negative they may have been, seeing them for what they were and releasing them cleanses this chakra. You may find yourself reliving bitter memories at the most unexpected moments while working on this. This is a natural reaction, and is very similar to the reaction of your stomach to unhealthy foods. It is a necessary cleansing process—an elimination of toxic memories and feelings.

Personal Examination

1. List four negative childhood experiences which happened to you, and the persons involved: parent, relative,

man, woman, another child. Make a similar list of four positive experiences.

2. Carefully consider your two lists and the people involved. Relate these early experiences to the opinions you now have, and to the ways you now react to certain situations and people.

3. Choose one past negative event. Study how it has conditioned you to respond negatively to situations. During meditation, visualize the event and the person or persons involved surrounded by white light. This is symbolic language to the subconscious mind, telling it to release and heal the memory.

4. Take inventory of your wants, needs, and goals. How do they fit into your four houses of responsibility? Can you keep these houses in balance and still achieve what you desire? If not, meditate upon a revision of your desires. Sometimes the smallest change in plans will put you in balance, and enable you to remove blockages from specific chakras.

The Spleen Chakra

The second center is in the middle of the lower abdominal region, and is associated with the physical spleen. It is connected with the transforming of lower vibrational energy into higher types of energy. This light center controls mental attitudes, and directly affects the physical body. If blocked, the ability to balance the life is impaired. This light center is a clear orange.

The adrenal glands, a pair of ductless glands, influence the spleen chakra. One gland sits near the top of each kidney, and produces hormones for metabolic actions, and adrenaline for the sympathetic nervous system. Mental attitudes, such as maturity, judgment, and control-urges are motivated by this light center. When the root and spleen centers are in balance, there is harmony between the physical body and the mind. If this chakra is blocked, or is never properly developed, all aspects of mental health are affected. The person lacks commonsense judgment, and is immature in personal relationships. He or she exhibits an urge to control other people, and reacts in a variety of ways, ranging from childish withdrawal to temper tantrums, in order to force people to accept his or her domination.

The spleen chakra has a direct and powerful influence upon the vitality of the astral body, and it enables a person to consciously astral travel. If underdeveloped, these travels are only vague memories. When problems arise in this center, or when a person is first making an effort to remove blockages here, it is common to experience dreams of flying or soaring through the air. Dreams of running away or trying to escape from someone or something are also quite common when dealing with past or present problems relating to the spleen or solar plexus chakras (third chakra). It is not unusual for a person who has experienced a traumatic childhood loss to find blockages in the first three light centers. The blockage may even go as far as the heart chakra. Those who have undergone an early shock of this nature tend to either cut spiritual learning out of their lives altogether, or search endlessly through many religions for spiritual satisfaction. They don't realize that, unless the blockages are faced and removed, they will never be satisfied with their lives.

An afflicted mental attitude will eventually create physical illness. Problems in this light center will be exhibited in varying degrees of nervousness, eczema and other hard-to-cure skin rashes; or, if other chakras are also involved, illnesses ranging from ulcers (particularly duodenal) to lower back problems. Kidney infections, stones, and constipation are strongly connected with the release of problems which are causing blockage in this chakra.

Personal Examination

1. Examine the lists you made with regard to this chakra. Can you identify any physical or mental illness in any of the negatives?

2. Can you see how any of your positive experiences could aid you in overcoming the negatives?

3. Since past negative experiences cause blockages and affect how *you* react to present events, it will be natural to see the same reaction in other people. Relate these behavior patterns between you and your spouse or mate, your children, your close friends, or your business associates to past experiences, if you know them.

The Solar Plexus Chakra

The third chakra is in the center of the abdomen at the navel. It is called the solar plexus, or navel chakra. This area of the body contains vast bundles of vital nerves, and joins other nerve bundles near the heart chakra. This light center is called the "second brain" of the body by mystics, and is sometimes called the "lower mind." It is a bright, clear yellow.

This light center deals with raw emotions, especially anger and frustration, and the intuition or gut feelings. As the center of empathy and identification, this chakra is strongly influenced by emotions. Properly developed, it can be trained to sense the emotions, desires, and intellectual levels of others without becoming involved. Positive work with this chakra generates understanding, patience, knowledge of who you are, self-control of emotions, and sympathy, but not pity, for others. People who refuse to show emotion or love, or those who show it to extremes, have definite problems in this chakra.

Blockage creates uncontrolled emotions, an inability to tap into the intuition, tenseness, and a lot of stomach problems. Uncontrolled or blocked, this light center radiates anger, false pride, jealousy, greed, resentment, and impatience. False intellectual pride is a common emotion seen in connection with blockage of this light center. If you put great emphasis on how much schooling you have and refuse to believe that anything else can be learned from someone with less formal education, you put a block in this chakra, and hinder spiritual development. Your search for truth must never stop.

This chakra is extremely sensitive, especially to the emotions projected by others. It is usually the first to be affected by psychic impressions and development. On the psychic and astral levels, development of this chakra awakens a sensitivity to all kinds of astral phenomena. Discernment of spirit must be practiced as this center begins to work more freely. A discernment of spirit is being aware of which astral entities are positive and which are negative.

In the physical body, the pancreas, with its islands of Langerhans, corresponds to this chakra. The islands of Langerhans affect the production of insulin and the secretion of digestive juices in the intestines. Physical illnesses commonly associated with blockages of this chakra are colds and flu (also associated with the throat chakra), stomach ulcers, and insomnia. As this light center begins to function more on a psychic level, intense emotions radiated from other people will feel like a physical blow to the abdomen. Your body has an automatic, subconscious response to this psychic battering; you will probably find yourself crossing your arms over this chakra in self-defense without ever thinking about what you are doing.

Living or working in close association with people who project heavily out of the second and third chakras can be a devastating daily experience, even when you are aware of what is happening. If responsibilities dictate your continued association with these people, be especially sure to make more quiet meditation time for yourself.

Personal Examination

1. Do you have any physical illnesses which relate to blockages in this particular chakra?

2. Can you trace the illness to the experience which created the blockage?

3. Put the persons involved, or the event itself, into the white light during meditation. Find at least one good thing which came out of the experience.

4. Use the following affirmation once a day until you feel release from the negative experience and the people involved:

   > *I am a special creation of the Goddess/God. I am balanced in body, mind, and spirit. There are no limits binding me to where and who I am.*

The Heart Chakra

The upper center of the chest is the seat of the heart chakra. Its color is a beautiful, clear, forest green, not the yellow-green or off-color green sometimes depicted.

The thymus gland, which lies in the upper chest region near the throat, is connected with this chakra. The thymus gland contributes to growth patterns, bone formation, blood production, and sexual development in the early years. Its malfunction causes very definite malignant diseases. This chakra affects unconditional spiritual love, compassion, empathy, and awareness of the oneness of all things. This center deals with the higher emotions of humans on a subjective level. Compassion, higher forms of love (especially spiritual love), self-respect, and incentive for self-improvement all develop here. It also affects the general prosperity of your life.

The development and an unblocked state of this chakra affects the astral body by attracting past-life lovers and acquaintances who were of positive quality. A blockage will attract those from past lives who were of negative quality. If blocked, one experiences self-hatred, distrust of others, and no understanding of the oneness of all creation. A disruption here creates an imbalance between the cold intellect and the physical drives. People who give their love only as a reward to those who obey them generally have congestion or difficulty in this area. These attitudes create diseases of the heart and lungs in the physical body.

Correctly balanced, this chakra gives us the ability to understand the vibrations of others on an astral level, and in turn projects our own higher feelings for understanding. When first learning to work out of this light center, it is common to reproduce within your own body the aches and pains of others around you because of misdirected sympathy. Development and balance of the heart chakra is the first real step on the spiritual path. Clearing and developing the first three chakras makes it possible to be a healthier, happier individual, but does not necessarily mean any further steps toward spiritual enlightenment will be taken. Persons who manage to balance the chakras to this point will clearly know who they are and what they want to do with life.

In people who take no interest in spirituality and personal self-improvement, this state of affairs will last until about the mid-forties. At that age, dissatisfaction will set in. It is not uncommon for people to jump into a heavy social life and extramarital affairs at this point. This restlessness, combined with activities which are harmful and certainly not progressive in any way, will begin to have a reverse effect on the very light centers they managed to keep open all those years. One by one, as the chakras become cluttered, physical illnesses will set in. The remainder of the person's lifetime will be one of physical dis-ease, constant bitter complaint, and progressively negative attitudes toward life itself.

Cleansing and balancing the heart chakra puts a definite flexibility of thought, and therefore of body, into a person's life. Bodily aging slows to the point where it seems to stop; mental faculties stay sharp.

Personal Examination

1. If a person or situation keeps your life in an uproar, it must be taken care of through the heart chakra, or spiritual love. Decide what your responsibilities are, if any. Determine what positive steps you can take to remedy the problem. Be sure you are not avoiding handling your end of the situation, or subconsciously hanging onto and feeding the continued upheaval.

2. If people trap you by using the "feel sorry for me" technique, consider if this falls into one of your houses of responsibility. If you accept their problems, will it throw your four personal responsibilities out of balance?

The Throat Chakra

At the bottom of the throat near the thyroid gland lies the throat chakra, known as the gateway to the spiritual "being-ness" of humans. The thyroid gland, situated just behind the larynx, is the ductless gland involved with this chakra. In the physical body, this gland secretes a hormone which stimulates basal metabolism. The color of this chakra is electric blue.

When fully developed and used, the throat chakra becomes the center of devotional and mystical ideas. Traditionally, it is the seat of communication, the balance of positive and negative, creativity of an abstract nature (art, literature, and music), and clairaudience (psychic hearing). Balanced, a person has a pleasant voice and speaks positively. Those who love to sing usually have a well-developed throat chakra. Unbalanced, it produces a sharp tongue, self-righteousness, and a closed mind.

The etheric sense, called clairaudience, corresponds to physical hearing, but doesn't necessarily work as an audible reception of sound. If an actual sound does carry over to the physical ear, it most commonly happens during that in-between state experienced when not quite awake. Etheric or astral sounds, voices, and music are heard through the throat chakra.

This chakra deals with the spiritual self-image, higher loyalties, and relating to the Goddess/God and other people as children of Goddess/God. It is from this center that we vocalize in positive or negative terms, and thus create events and conditions in our bodies and surroundings. It is very important to learn to watch what you say. Constant, repeated verbalization of ideas creates images first in the mind, then in the body, then in life situations around you. If you keep expressing negative ideas, they will become physical facts. The vocalized word is extremely powerful. I've known people who repeatedly refer to others (usually those who won't submit to their control) as a "pain in the neck." These people suffer from frequent neck problems and headaches. The power of this chakra can be harnessed for constructive use only by watching your words. By purposely using positive, constructive words about a person or a situation which is causing trouble, you can create a change for the good. This may occur through changing the attitude of the person, or the situation, to a positive pole of energy, or by removing the person or situation from your life altogether. A harsh verbal argument with another person can create, within a few hours' time, such illnesses as laryngitis, colds, flu, and other irritations of the nose, throat, and sinuses. Angry conditions, in which you would like to say something in retort but don't, also cause a congestion in this chakra. Tonsillitis, mastoiditis, and other similar ailments are the result of harsh words, even if they are not said aloud.

Often we are in a position where saying something would put us in danger of, for instance, physical harm or loss of job. Vocally expressing angry feelings often causes chakra blockage, a problem far more troublesome than remaining quiet. Try, instead, to find a personal way to release your anger. A woman I know spits repeatedly into the toilet, visualizing the troublesome person going down the drain when she flushes. Positive words and affirmations have great healing power. It is for this reason that only positive, healing words should be used around people who have dis-ease in the physical body. Although a person who has lapsed into a coma may not seem to hear, he or she actually does hear every word on a subconscious level.

Personal Examination

1. If you suffer occasional sore throats, colds, sinus problems, ear infections, or similar physical ailments, can

you link these to incidents of anger, either expressed or unexpressed?

2. Is your problem that of frequent vocal battles, or does the problem involve not saying what you would like to say? Find a physical method which enables you to release the anger.

3. Be as impersonal as possible in determining how to handle such aggravating incidents. Be sure to consider your four areas of responsibility in your decisions.

4. For one week, be aware of what words you use frequently. Do you use negative words, like "feel sorry for," "can't afford," "always goes wrong," or "I hate"? Substitute such phrases as "I choose not to purchase that now," "this is only a minor setback," or "I dislike."

The Brow Chakra

The sixth, or brow chakra is located in the center of the forehead between, and a little above, the eyebrows. The ductless pineal gland, associated with this chakra, appears to regulate brain development and the physical body's ability to use light rays. This center is often called the "third eye," or the "transcendent gateway," and is seen as a bluish-purple color.

Higher psychic phenomena, such as etheric color perception, spiritual intuition, true clairvoyance, and healing, come through this chakra. You can train yourself to "see" through this chakra; you may even encounter the vision of a great eye staring back at you in meditation when this center begins to work. In its connection with the pituitary gland, it affects clear-seeing and psychic perception in all its forms.

Clairvoyance enables you to sense the shape and nature of astral objects and entities. In early development, this psychic talent comes through as half-seen landscapes, disembodied faces, and clouds of color. When you use clairvoyance you are actually looking psychically into the brow chakra. In fact, you will be able to see better and clearer if you close your physical eyes and look within.

Developing the brow chakra increases the correct use of will power, the faith, and the spiritual understanding of the individual. (By faith, I don't mean the term used by orthodox religions to mean accepting whatever you are told without question; I am referring to believing in things which can't be physically seen or proved.) Guidance and direction of personal will power in a positive manner, so important for fully developing all the chakras, is originated and perfected here.

This chakra deals heavily with intuitive, spiritual understanding, which is so important for physical, mental, emotional, and particularly spiritual progress. Intuitive understanding can only be acquired by regular periods of quiet study and meditation. When this chakra is correctly balanced, you can instantly see through to the truth of any situation. Developed spiritual understanding is a must for anyone who works with psychic healing. Many times the healer must reach with the intuition to find the real root of a physical illness or problem. An example is cancer. As in many diseases, cancer creates an actual physical disturbance of the body; however, the cancer itself is built out of layers of thought patterns. Layers and layers of dark, troubled thoughts of fear, unforgiveness, rebellion, rage, and discouragement create a disturbance or short-circuit in the body cells, which in turn creates the cancer. In reality cancer is nothing more than misdirected cells which have forgotten what their relationship to the body is supposed to be.

Problems with understanding clutter the brow chakra, and can cause headaches, muscle spasms in the neck and shoulders, problems in the legs, feet and knees, deafness, and eye diseases. The feet and legs are the foundation upon which the physical human stands; intuitive spiritual understanding is the basis of the spiritual human.

Personal Examination

1. Visualize the light centers or chakras of your body, beginning with the root chakra and working up to the crown of the head. Picture each as a balloon of the correct color in the correct location in the astral body. As you visualize each light center, ask to be shown any blockages which may be there. End the visualization by surrounding yourself with white light.

2. Begin to keep a dream journal, writing down dreams you remember, and dating each. No matter how fragmentary your recollections, record them. Check carefully to see if the symbols used in the dreams relate to problems in the chakras. These may be either existing blockages or potential ones because of problems with new experiences.

The Crown Chakra

The seventh light center is at the crown of the head near the pineal gland. It is the ultimate chakra, and the last to fully open. It connects you directly to Goddess/God and, when open, produces a halo-like effect. The Hindus call it the "Lotus of the Thousand Petals." This center synchronizes all the others, integrates all polarities, and is all-pervading in its power. Humans do not operate with the crown chakra open constantly. Its color is a delicate lavender, but can become a gleaming white with a golden heart in the very spiritually advanced.

The pituitary gland governing this chakra secretes a number of hormones, which control a variety of body functions, including the other ductless glands. It controls body growth and metabolic functions, regulates pigmentation and cell-stimulation, and acts directly on kidney and uterine functions. The crown chakra works closely with the brow chakra. Full activity of both the crown and brow chakras are found only in a few highly-developed people who have complete enlightenment in all chakras on all levels. They are able to leave the body in full consciousness whenever they so desire, and return, sometimes after an astral journey of hours or days. When physical death comes, they can exit in full consciousness without fear, knowing that there is no difference between this final journey and the astral journeys with which they are so familiar.

All the chakras appear in the astral body as slight depressions because they are constantly drawing in cosmic energy. However, as the crown chakra becomes developed and begins changing from violet to white, the depression changes to a rounded projection at the top of the head. At this point in spiritual development, there is as much or more sending out of cosmic energy from the crown chakra as there is intake in the other chakras. This radiation of light from this light center is portrayed as halos in Western art and the rounded head-dome in Eastern art.

When this chakra begins to develop, there will be new insight and understanding of old problems. Blockages become more apparent and more easily removed. The crown chakra affects the development of psychic abilities and spiritual attainment. If clear, its energy will attract high-level teachers and even deities when you are out on the astral planes.

Personal Examination

1. Check back on the lists you made at the beginning of these exercises. How many of the negative experiences have you changed to positive?

2. Meditate on your seven chakras. What new positive powers have you found in each one?

3. Prove to yourself the power of your words. Select a situation or problem in your life which you feel needs to be resolved, and correlate it to the proper chakra. Cleanse your chakras as described later in this chapter. Return mentally to the chosen chakra and flood it with the proper color while thinking of a positive solution. End by visualizing yourself surrounded by white light. In your daily life, speak only positive words about the situation or problem.

Cleansing the Aura and the Light Centers

Since the aura of a human's astral body reflects the condition of the chakras, it is essential that both the aura and the chakras be cleaned periodically. It is also true that any contamination picked up by the aura from other beings (physical or astral) will make its way from the aura into the light centers.

Every astral traveler, indeed every serious student, should cleanse and regenerate his or her light centers on a regular basis. This can easily be done with thirty seconds of carefully controlled deep breathing, either in direct sunlight or in mentally created white light. This dramatically affects the appearance of the chakras, changing the physical, mental, emotional, and spiritual bodies and attitudes. This cleansing enables the chakras to draw greater amounts of energy molecules out of the air and convert them to usable physical and psychic energy, replenishing all the bodies, seen and unseen.

Before attempting to cleanse your aura, you should cleanse and rebalance your chakras. If you have studied the chakras, and gone through the personal examination at the end of each section, you have completed the first step of the cleansing. The second step of chakra cleansing requires a pendulum and small squares or circles to match each chakra color. Photography supply houses sell sheets of colored plastic which are excellent for this. Cut a square of each color, no larger than two by two inches. Always begin with the root chakra red, moving up through each chakra, until you reach the crown. Place the red square in the palm of one hand. Hold the pendulum in your power hand over the colored square. The pendulum will begin to swing in a clockwise direction as energy is absorbed. Sometimes it will take a long time for the pendulum to stop; when this happens, you are very low on root chakra energy, or are out of balance there. Other times the pendulum will swing only a brief time, showing that you do not need much cleansing in this chakra at this time.

Lay aside the red square and take up the orange one. Repeat the process with the pendulum. Continue in order through each of the chakras, until you finish with the crown lavender. Your chakras are now balanced as much as possible. Any further balancing must be done by mentally ridding each center of old, negative baggage.

Aura cleansing can be done in several ways, depending upon whether you have unlimited time, or are pressed for privacy and time. If you feel an urgent need to clean your aura, and have little if any privacy, you can retreat to a bathroom by yourself. Using your hands, make sweeping motions over your body from the head to the feet. As you complete each pass, flick your hands as if ridding them of water. Finish by surrounded yourself with visualized white light. This method is quite good if you know your aura has just been contaminated by someone else's aura, or by something left in an atmosphere by a person who is no longer there.

If you have plenty of time and privacy to clean your aura, sit quietly and close your eyes. Visualize giant hands sweeping down through your aura, scraping off all the astral gunk which has accumulated. Take as long as you need to feel clean again. Next, see these hands gently pulling each chakra color down over your body, beginning with red and ending with lavender. Finish by visualizing white light completely surrounding you.

Blockages can occur at any time, if you do not maintain an awareness. Do a periodic reexamination of your aura and chakras. Take any discovered problems immediately into meditation for impersonal, intuitive understanding. Strive to maintain a balance of your four responsibilities; and remember, your goal of greater spiritual awareness should not, and cannot, be gained at the expense of anyone else, or you will short-circuit your own attempts.

There are definite reasons for aura and chakra cleansing besides keeping you healthy on all levels: It also creates a proper and acceptable energy field for attracting a higher-level astral lover. No matter how you start out in your astral adventures, sooner or later you will desire an astral love experience. Even if you should have a constant astral lover-companion, eventually your spiritual growth will propel you toward communication with higher-level entities. Chakra-melding with a high-level being is a special spiritual occasion, one completely devoid of the usual sexual overtones, but an event not to be avoided if you are offered the opportunity.

Six

∞

Hello and Good-bye

B y this stage of your development and practice, you probably have an astral companion or lover. Life is improving for you on all levels; you have help accomplishing your goals, moving about on the astral planes, practicing psychic talents, and advancing spiritually. You no longer feel unloved, alone, or undesirable. What more could you learn about astral lovers? Well, actually quite a lot. One of the next things you should know is how to release ties with one astral lover and attract a new one.

It is possible that at some time you may want to break the relationship with an astral lover and seek out a new one. Most relationships on the astral planes are little different than relationships on the physical plane. Some are permanent and long-term, while others sour in a short time. Most fall in-between: they are neither breath-stopping, nor are they hell to live in; they just become dull, monotonous, and uninspiring.

Perhaps this desire for change occurs because you made a bad choice. Perhaps the astral being in question did a good con job and made you believe they were other than they are.

Perhaps your needs and expectations have changed, and you've grown spiritually to the point where the two of you no longer have much to offer each other. Usually a polite discussion with your astral lover is enough to conclude the relationship. You may well find that the astral lover also has been contemplating the end of the relationship. Ideally, those on the astral plane are growing and evolving just as we should be. You may even be shocked to learn that your astral lover is eager to terminate the relationship because he or she considers you a detriment to *his or her* growth. This can happen particularly if you have allowed your life to slide downhill morally and spiritually. Be as graceful as you would expect them to be; don't wail, cry, or whine. Above all, don't become a nuisance, following the ex-lover around on the astral, and snooping into his or her next relationship. Ask if he or she will tell you what you need to do to grow—not with the idea of getting back together, but in preparation for another, better astral relationship with another being. Most importantly, listen when they tell you.

If you were not careful in selecting your astral lover, you may have entered a relationship with a being who is clinging, possessive, or has a tendency to become a nuisance if thwarted. The possibility of this happening becomes stronger if you have a tendency toward the same types of physical relationships. To determine if you have this tendency, don't look at your love relationships, but at your friendships with both men and women. Do you allow yourself to be sucked into friendships with people with whom you later have problems? Do the same problems appear again and again, only with different people? Do you drift in and out of friendships, never really giving very much of yourself? Do you give too much of yourself, trying to please everyone? If you have a friend who constantly disparages you in subtle ways, do you just bite your tongue and take it, or do you say what you think? Do you allow such friendships to continue even when you reach the point of avoiding the person? Do you try to chum with the "in crowd" so you can feel popular? Do you force yourself on people or groups where you really are not wanted? If you answer yes to more than one of these questions, you need to do some serious work on yourself. Return to Chapter Five and reread the section on chakras. Go through the personal examinations again, and be truthful! Cleanse your aura and chakras regularly, and begin taking responsibility for whom you allow around you as friends.

When you feel you are beginning to have better control over yourself; when you feel you are beginning to attract a better quality of friend; this is the time to end old astral relationships and move on to new ones. You may want or need to sever contact with an astral being before this, but under no circumstances should you try to establish a new astral relationship until you have mastered your own problems.

Depending upon the type of astral being with whom you have had the relationship, you may or may not have to go through a series of steps in order to sever the tie. There are several effective techniques for releasing astral lovers. If you chose a being from the middle levels of the astral planes, ending the relationship will not be a problem. Use the following meditation to your special astral place to tell your astral lover that the relationship is now ended. You may well arrive at your special place to find a message stating that your lover cannot meet you, and that he or she also wishes to end the relationship with no ill feelings.

Releasing Meditation

Prepare as usual for your meditation: quiet place where you will not be disturbed, soft non-vocal music, phone shut off, pets out of the room, and a comfortable chair. Sit in a comfortable position and visualize yourself surrounded by the white light. Relax your body completely, beginning with your feet and legs and working up to your neck and head. Visualize yourself standing beside a deep well. Mentally take all the negatives in your life (this includes people) and drop them into the well. Don't worry about what happens to them or watch them fall. Just turn and walk away.

Think of your special astral place, the one you built at the beginning of this book, and you will instantly be there. Walk through this place, enjoying the ocean, lake, mountains, or whatever Nature setting you created. Feel yourself becoming more relaxed and calm. Go to your sacred pool and kneel beside the quiet water. Call up the white light and visualize its brilliance around you. Breathe it in slowly until you feel it penetrate every cell of your physical and astral bodies. Now look at your reflection in the pool. When you see your third eye in the center of your forehead begin to swirl, think of ending your astral relationship. Project this thought through your third eye and let it fall into the water. Reach out and push it gently under, smoothing the ripples with your hands. Wish your astral lover well; if you harbor negative feelings about the situation, you will only strengthen whatever ties are between you.

Rise and go to your nearby astral "home," the one you built and furnished with everything you desired. Dress yourself in something beautiful and comfortable. Prepare drinks of some kind and set them beside two close chairs. Then think of your astral lover and ask him or her to join you. At this point, you may receive a mental message such as "I know the relationship is over. Best wishes and be happy." If this is the case, sit and relax with your drink before you return to the physical.

It is more likely, however, that your astral lover will appear, knowing, of course, what is on your mind. As the two of you sit sipping your drinks, you will need to telepathically send the message that you want the relationship to end. Your lover may well point out things you should know about yourself and your subconscious motives. Listen closely, for your lover (if the sincere kind) will be telling you the truth to help you make better choices in the future. At the end of the conversation, the astral lover will leave.

On some occasions, particularly if you made a bad choice in astral lovers, you will find yourself with a very sticky situation on your hands. The lover may whine, threaten, rage, or actually try to attack you. In this case, immediately throw a shield of white light around you to prevent any contact. Shout for your teachers and the astral police; they will remove the offending astral entity and protect you.

Sometimes you will experience an in-between situation where the astral lover will neither exit gracefully nor try to force you to change your mind. He or she will beg, try to make you feel wrong and guilty, promise to do anything. Stand by your decision. Any person, astral or physical, is highly unlikely to make the kind of drastic personality changes promised at a time like this. Don't get sucked into the sympathy game. Be polite but firm. End the relationship and ask him or her to leave.

When you are finished with this emotional severing, go at once to your astral temple. Sit in your chair before the altar. Call upon the Supreme Deity by whatever name you use. Sit there until you begin to feel calm and collected again. Now go to your healing table with the overhead lights. Undress and lie on the table, as the lights bathe you in soft blue and pink glowing radiance. Finally, the lights become a brilliant white, cleansing your aura and sealing any breaks in it. When you are finished with the healing treatment, think of your physical body and return to it. Sit quietly for several minutes while you think about what has happened.

If you experienced a scene with your astral lover not wanting to terminate the relationship, you will need to take other measures to be certain that the unhappy being does not continue to hang around. If he or she was the whining, begging kind, you need only avoid contact for several weeks—both in your thoughts and in your astral travels. Usually this entity will give up and go away. To help the situation, perform a brief candle-burning ritual with a pink candle. Hold the candle in both hands and think of the ex-lover as moving out of your vibrations, and finding a new person with whom to be happy. Wish him or her well, then light the candle and let it burn completely out.

If the astral lover threatened or showed any form of violence toward you, you need to be very careful, and take decisive steps to protect yourself. First, you should avoid deliberate astral travel for at least six weeks. Second, to protect yourself while astral traveling during sleep, wear a piece of protective jewelry, such as an amulet, talisman, special pendant, or ring. Consecrate these for protection by passing them through patchouli incense smoke. Usually, burning a pink candle for these negative, violent types of astral entities has no effect. You might try a deep purple candle; however, you will probably have to resort to a black candle. Mentally pour into the candle the thoughts that the entity cannot enter your vibration, cannot harm you, cannot affect your life in any way. See a strong, high, thick mental wall between the two of you. Light the candle and let it burn out completely, and throw the wax away. Regardless of how your astral lover behaves, and especially if you received a negative reaction, cleanse your aura and rebalance your chakras daily for a week.

Before trying to attract another astral lover, go back through the lists you created in Chapter Two. Redo the lists, correcting and raising your expectations. Go through each of the meditations connected with each list. Redo the chakra and aura-cleansing techniques, being very attentive to what happens during these times. You really need to change yourself and your desires before getting involved with another astral lover. When you feel you are ready to meet another lover, begin the relationship as you should have done with the first one. Insist upon a friendship and courtship period first. Get to know this astral being thoroughly, spending as much time as possible talking with each other. Ask your teacher-guides what they think about your new astral companion, and if they disagree with your choice, listen carefully to the reasons they give and think them over seriously. You may even find that one of your teachers is the astral lover for whom you have been searching.

The following meditation will help you attract a positive astral companion, if you have done all your homework.

Attracting Meditation

Prepare yourself as usual for your meditation. If you use incense, set it far enough away that you won't be bothered by the smoke. If you decide to light a white light, put it in a safe place where you will not knock it over by accident. Begin by sitting in a comfortable position and visualizing yourself surrounded by the white light. Relax your body completely, beginning with your feet and legs and working up to your neck and head. Take as much time as you need for this, but don't dwell on whether or not you are relaxed.

Visualize yourself standing beside a deep well. Mentally take all the negatives in your life (this includes people) and drop them into the well. Don't worry about what happens to them or watch them fall. When you are finished, turn and walk away. Think of your special astral place and you will instantly be there. Walk through this place and feel yourself becoming more relaxed and calm.

If you wish to attract an astral lover from the middle levels who will comfort and help you with your physical life, enter your astral home and prepare for the meeting. You may wish to have drinks, something to eat, special music, or other similar treats. Of course you will want to present yourself in the best possible light. Remember, on the astral planes you can create any outfit you want to wear, including jewelry and other accessories. Prepare yourself as you would for any first date.

When you have everything ready, send out a mental invitation for astral beings who meet your desires and needs. Don't be surprised if more than one such being shows up. There is no hurry to make a choice (if you ever do); after all, you are planning to have a friendship, followed by courtship, and this all takes time. Talk with your prospective suitors, listening to what they say and how they say it. Watch their auras for unusual flares or off-colored spots. Occasionally, powerful low-level entities will try to sneak in, but you should have no difficulty spotting such entities and requesting that they leave immediately. If one does manage to remain unnoticed by you, one of the other astral beings will point out the potential troublemaker within a short time.

It is a prudent move to invite your teacher-guides to this get-together also. Their mere presence sometimes causes an undesirable entity to leave immediately upon discovery. You can be certain that the retreating astral being was not one with whom you want to become involved. When your party is over, thank everyone for being with you. Think of your physical body and you will return to it at once.

Carefully consider what happened during this meditation. It helps to write down your impressions about each astral being who came. Did they say anything about being with you in other lifetimes? What occupation are they pursuing on the astral? What did your teachers have to say about each one? Take your time before choosing one or more astral lovers. Never rush into relationships. If an astral being begins to pressure you for more intimate contact before you feel ready, cut the ties and end the relationship. Never be pressured into anything you don't want to do, and don't feel ready to experience. You have every right to be particular about your astral companions and lovers. The higher your spiritual goals, the better astral lover you will attract.

Spend several weeks, or even months, enjoying the companionship of one or more astral entities before making any decisions about advancing the relationship. During this time period, keep working on yourself and your attitudes. Cleanse your aura and rebalance your chakras often.

Seven

∞

Multiple Chakra Melding

For centuries there have been debates (usually among men) about the possibility of loving more than one person at a time. Although it isn't a common occurrence, it *is* possible to love more than one person at the same time. I'm not saying this is desirable, undesirable, or sinful; I'm only saying it's possible. In physical-plane relationships this will only cause you heaps of trouble, and is best avoided. The astral planes are totally different.

Although you should keep your ethics high to avoid low-level astral entities, you may find yourself in an astral situation where you love, and are loved by, two or more astral entities of good quality. Sometimes these beings are gracious enough to allow you to enjoy their company in turn—rather like dating two considerate, loving humans. Other times you may find yourself in a loving, passionate experience with both at the same time. Ordinarily, this *ménage à trois* situation occurs when your astral lovers feel that you need the energy of them both to build power for a manifestation you desire, break loose some resistant chakra blockages, undergo a healing, or

129

as a preparation for more advanced group chakra-melding. It can also occur when you are going through a very devastating, personal time which has left you depressed, despondent, and generally feeling as worthless as last week's garbage. In this case, you will be receiving far more love and healing energy than you are sharing with your lovers. Relax and soak it up. They will understand.

Astral Ménage à Trois

When chakra-melding occurs among three or more entities, the chakras exchange energy much as they do between two beings. However, these lines of power amplify and re-amplify as they travel between you and your lovers. For example, your throat chakra would send out a beam of connecting energy to both astral partners. Each of their throat chakras would connect not only with you, but with each other. Then the brow and crown chakras connect. As this rush of high-level energy pours through your body, each of the lower chakras will connect. The resultant inflow and outflow of energy continues to build. The chakras blaze so clear and clean, that you are bathed in an overwhelming rainbow of brilliant colors. It is an experience that takes the word pleasure right off the scale of human understanding. It can be ecstasy such as you have never known before. This powerful experience can even cause your physical body to quiver. Be mentally prepared, for such a melding can cause a physical orgasm.

You most certainly can't be a sexual prude if you undergo this intense experience. You can't be thinking what a sinful person you are while your astral lovers are trying to meld chakras with you. If you do, you will short-circuit the whole experience. Your lovers will understand your reservations the first time they approach you with a suggestion for multiple chakra-melding. They will do their best to make you feel at ease by answering your questions, and by not pushing or coercing you into participating if you feel unready. If and when you do go through this experience with your lovers, you will find yourself discarding a lot of outworn, constricting, and controlling propaganda you learned as a child. This doesn't mean you will be out flashing your bare bottom in the streets, or taking part in a physical *ménage à trois* to prove you are now liberated; it does mean that you will take a more moderate attitude toward what others do (after all, you don't live their lives or pay their bills), and will definitely question a lot of unasked-for orthodox propaganda.

An example of how this experience of multiple chakra-melding can benefit you is if you are experiencing a very low period in your life: Your love life has gone sour or is nonexistent; your body is rebelling through illness; or your whole life is on a downhill plunge. You feel unloved, weak, depressed, and generally miserable, and you just can't seem to get up the energy to project anything positive to turn your life around.

Your astral lovers are aware of your problems, and invite you to share a multiple chakra-melding with them. They are very gentle, allowing you to be as passive as you wish. They put their arms around you, and the chakras begin to meld, the energy to flow. Your psychic batteries begin to recharge. You soak up their energy and love, and revel in it. Soon your chakras begin to give as well as take. The power increases. By the time your lovers return you to the physical world, you feel able to face life again.

If your physical life experiences have been particularly negative, or if you have been in a slump for a long period of time, it will take several multiple chakra-melding sessions before you feel better and can stay that way upon your return.

Suppose, though, that you feel great and have no pressing need for such a tremendous lift of spirit. What good is multiple chakra-melding then? By agreement with your lovers, you can channel that energy into producing a desired manifestation for yourself or another. You must all agree that manifesting the desire will not harm another person, and will be a positive experience for you, or the person for whom you are working. Then, while the chakra-melding is occurring, you must center your thoughts on the fully visualized event you wish to manifest. The stronger the chakra-melding becomes, the more powerful the energy sent to the manifestation, and the harder it is to concentrate. (This same technique can be used during physical lovemaking. The participating partners must agree upon what they wish to manifest, then concentrate on sending the power raised into that manifestation. At the point of orgasm, the power is released. This is much easier said than done, which is why sex magick is considered to be a difficult, highly advanced use of magick.)

Group Chakra Melding for the Benefit of Others

People who are into magick like to meet in groups, where they can raise more energy to project toward a physical manifestation to help an individual, a country, or the world. The majority of these groups don't use group sex magick, but rather regular magickal proceedings. High-level astral beings often meet in such groups for specific purposes, using group chakra-melding to raise a type of sexual astral energy. This energy is then poured into a specific desire to be manifested.

Although it is not a desirable experience for all astral travelers, it is possible for humans to participate in group chakra-melding and magick on the astral planes. One has to be extremely careful when considering getting involved in such activities, since there are many low-level sexual addicts who operate on the belief "the more the merrier." High-level astral group sexual magick is not performed for sexual gratification. True spiritual connections with a group of high-level entities is very powerful, and is the only kind in which you should become involved. These higher entities are using their sexual emotions to raise power, mold it into a desired form, and send it out for manifestation in the physical world, for anything from spiritual awakening for whole human groups or areas of people, to world peace. There are always reasons for this group activity beyond cheap thrills. They are quick to exclude and evict any interloping sexual thrill-seekers or astral travelers who are there just to feed off the fringes of their raised energy. Before you ever think about joining such a group event, you must know yourself and all your obvious and hidden motives. The following short test will help you to determine if you are ready for such powerful magick.

Self-Evaluation Test

1. What are your actual, true expectations from such a group experience?

2. Are you attracted because of the unique sexual-type event? The quality of the participants? The fact that it sounds exciting?

3. How did you encounter this magickal group? Accidentally came upon them? Crashed the event, either by yourself or with another astral entity? Were you invited?

4. You will meet some very high-powered, high-level astral entities in these groups. Could you associate with them without acting like a groupie? Would you be tongue-tied if one of them talked with you, or would you just be shy and very aware of your lack of knowledge?

5. If you are heterosexual, could you chakra-meld with an astral entity of your sex without reacting negatively? If you are homosexual, could you perform this function with an opposite-sex astral partner?

You also need to be very aware of the vibrations of every entity involved in the group activity. Most of the time all participants in such a group ritual (and it *is* a ritual) will be of a fairly high level, and will be there by the consent of all the others present. They have varying degrees of magickal skills, but are all united in the common cause of working for a specific outcome or manifestation.

Occasionally, when the other members are concentrating on what they plan to do, an uninvited entity can slip in. The really slimy, low-level entities are detected immediately, if they ever manage to get anywhere near the ritual proceedings. Their vibrations set off a mental alarm in any middle or high-level being. It is the borderline astral beings with some knowledge and magickal skill, or the devious, powerful negative ones, who can camouflage themselves enough to enter the fringes of such a circle. They tend to stay away from the high-level beings, who would unmask them in an instant. Instead, they look for beginners to this type of magick—astral travelers who are overwhelmed by what is going on, and who fail to remain aware and cautious.

Surely you have been to a party or a gathering where a stranger appeared and everyone assumed that someone else had invited him or her. At some point, someone realized that

the stranger was simply a party-crasher. Some of these uninvited people leave quietly upon discovery, while others have
to be carted away by the police. An example of a harmless
party-crasher (in a roundabout way) is what occurs frequently
in a certain city park near a mental hospital. The patients at
the hospital are neither violent nor dangerous, so there are no
high walls or guards. Ordinarily they roam about the
grounds, never going far. During the summer, however, the
city park is often the scene of large family reunions. A few of
the patients will then wander down into the park, get in line
for food, and enjoy themselves for the afternoon, until one of
the hospital personnel discovers they are gone and retrieves
them. Everyone at the family gathering assumes the patients
are family members they don't know. Since these "visiting"
patients love people, particularly children, and no one is ever
harmed in any way, there is no danger.

The same cannot be said about unknowns in a group performing astral sex magick. Other human astral travelers may
manage to get into the group, but most of these will have a
right to be there and will not be harmful. A few, however, will
be party-crashers who see an opportunity for sexual thrills. If
someone does not remove them, they will contaminate both
your personal aura and the magickal power raised. Many of
these entities were once human magicians who dabbled in
negative types of magick with evil intent. Some will have been
black magicians and Satanists. The best defense against the
dangers of encountering these entities is to attend such a
group upon invitation only. When your teachers think you
are ready for such an experience, an escort will be sent to take
you to the ritual and bring you back again. Stay near this
astral escort the whole time you are there, or at least until you
get the auric feel of the entities involved. You may feel a little
foolish at first, following your escort around like a shadow,

but that is safer than wandering off and getting your aura "tagged" by some unscrupulous party-crasher.

In accordance with the saying "as above, so below," there are also negative magickal groups on the astral who use sexual rituals. These are led by powerful, negative astral entities for their own perverse purposes. Often these groups are convened merely to attract novices in astral travel. Unless you are aware of the auras of these entities, you could get tricked into joining their proceedings. The power flow of chakra-melding between these astral entities is totally different from that felt during a ritual with high-level beings. These negative beings will meld from the root chakra to the solar plexus chakra, never higher. Once they get attached to your lower chakras, the root chakra in particular, they can return and reestablish the connection while you are sleeping. This was the origin of the evil *incubus* and *succubus*.

In physical magickal groups having members of both sexes, it is usual to alternate male and female around a circle, thus balancing the polarities of energy raised. On the astral, male does not necessarily mean male energy, or female, female energy. The terms, male and female, actually have little meaning on the astral planes, except as a kind of identification. You may find yourself projecting energy of the opposite sex to what you are while on the astral. You may discover that you project one type of energy one time, another type of energy another time. This has nothing to do with how you identify yourself sexually while in the physical.

For the first few times you visit such a working group, you may be asked to watch and not take part in the ritual. If you are invited to participate, feel honored and follow instructions. Some astral groups operate much as do earthly Pagan gatherings, while others are more like ceremonial magick. If you have an opportunity to do so, take part in both types.

Ordinarily a magickal ritual circle will be cast and consecrated the same, or nearly the same, as it is done in physical plane Wiccan or ceremonial magick proceedings. Then group members will stand in a close circle, facing the center. The entity who is leading the group will state what manifestation they will be working on. At a signal from this leader, the group will begin to meld throat or brow chakras. You will be able to see these intense lines of power going from one entity to another until all in the circle are connected. Then the melding rises to the next chakra, until the crown light center is reached.

When the chakra at the top of the head is connected, there will be a tremendous rush of visible power downward through all the lower chakras. The center of the circle will be one great mass of energy. You will be able to feel the type of energy it has become. The leader will call out, "release!" and everyone will disconnect, allowing the raised power to shoot away from the circle of entities. It will finish forming in the astral before it descends into the physical, where it will manifest into the desired form.

Meditation on a Group Ritual

Set up your usual physical preparations for meditation. Close your eyes and visualize the white light completely surrounding and protecting you. Relax your body from the feet up to the head, taking as much time as necessary, but not getting tense about how you are doing. Make your usual stop at the deep well to dispose of all the negatives in your life. Think of your special astral place and you will be there. Go to your sacred temple or worship place and sit in your chair before the altar. Your regular astral companion or lover, or one of your teachers will meet you there. If you have any questions or fears about this visit to a high-level magickal group, now is the time to discuss it with your lover or teacher. Take as much time as you feel you need.

As you relax before your altar, the temple begins to fill with swirling clouds of brilliant light. An astral entity comes into the temple and stops beside your chair. The feeling coming from this being is soothing and full of love. See if you can determine if this is a male or female—many high-level beings appear to be neither. You may be given a name; however, this will not be the name by which this being is known in astral magickal circles; it will simply be a way for you to address this high-level being without being reduced to saying "you" or to tugging at his or her robe for attention.

The high-level magician takes your hand and leaves the temple. Your teacher or lover may be asked to accompany you so you will not feel alone and uneasy. As you step through the temple door, you and your companions are immediately transported on a billowing iridescent cloud to another, higher level of the astral planes. You may find yourself in one of two places, depending upon the magickal path of the high-level beings who have called you. One meeting place is a beautiful, wide, forest clearing with tall, dark evergreens all around. It is night with a brilliant Full Moon above. Around the edges of the clearing are rough-hewn benches and tables. In the center of the clearing stands a large group of beings, robed in plain dark colors, softly singing while etheric music fills the air. Your guide to this place escorts you and your companions to one of the benches. You will be allowed to watch, but not participate this time. You may see other astral travelers along the edges of the clearing, who also have come to view this powerful ritual.

Your guide joins the other entities as they gather in a great circle. As they begin their ritual, you can see a large silver star standing upright on a stone altar in the exact center of the circle.

One of the entities sweeps the edges of the area with an old-fashioned broom, while another follows behind with a sword, blue flames remarking the boundary. Two of the entities—the leaders for this occasion—stand before the altar and bless vessels containing the water and salt, which they then sprinkle along the still-pulsating circle outline. They replace the vessels on the stone altar and join the main group.

As the high-level entities join hands and begin to chant, you feel the very air around you begin to change. The vibrations become so spiritual, so strong, that you feel almost euphoric. The chanting voices rise and fall on the still night air. An owl hoots in the trees behind you, while the singing cries of wolves come from a distance. The silver star on the altar begins to pulsate, then spin. Lines dart from one brow chakra to another around the circled beings. Then the crown chakras are connected. These lines of etheric energy are quite visible, forming a strange web pattern which fills in the circle, with the altar and star at its center. The star whirls faster, until it is a blur. As the energy moves from the crown chakras of the astral beings down through the rest of the chakras, the star rises from the altar to hang in the air over the encircled magicians. Everyone shouts a word which you can't quite understand. The star suddenly expands into a gigantic energy ball and disappears.

The leader of the group ritually breaks the circle outline with the sword, thus ending the ritual. The magicians move quietly to the benches along the edges of the clearing. Your guide returns to sit beside you. Beautiful plates of food and chalices of liquid are given to all. Those who took part in the ritual quickly drink, then hold their chalices up to be refilled. Show restraint on sampling the food and drink, for these are highly charged with astral power, and can quickly fill you with so much energy that you will be too charged to sleep for hours after your return to the physical plane.

The high-level being who guided you to this meeting place turns to you with a smile and asks if you have any questions. If you ask something you aren't supposed to know yet, your guide will politely tell you so. Several other beings who were in the magickal circle come over to talk with you and your companions. Your teacher asks if you have a project or desire you need manifested. If you do, a small group of the high-level beings, plus you and your teacher, form a circle. One of the astral entities casts and consecrates a small circle around the group, then they all join hands and ask you to visualize the outcome you desire. As you mentally picture what you want, a tiny star materializes on the stone altar. You feel your chakras connecting with the chakras of all those within the circle. Your companions begin to chant. Soon the instruction is given to loose the power. You let go of your mental picture, and it flies into the tiny star on the altar. The star shoots upward and disappears. The circle is ritually cut, and everyone joins the rest of the magicians.

After a few moments, your teacher takes your hand and says you must return to the physical. Instantly, you find yourself back in your astral home. Your teacher speaks with you for a few moments longer, then helps you to return to your physical body.

You can read the above meditation forever, but unless you experience the power formed by a group of high-level astral magicians, there is no way for you to understand what actually happens and how it feels. You may never wish to take part in such a group chakra-melding. The choice is always yours.

If you think you are in the right high-level group, but suddenly find one of the beings trying to connect with any of your lower chakras, break the contact at once and return to your body! Never accept any offers of friendship from any astral being hanging around the fringes of such a group without checking out their aura. It is also wise to double-check with your teacher about such an individual. Power attracts all kinds of astral beings; there well might be uninvited guests who are not of the highest quality.

The power raised during the group chakra-melding, in such a circle of high-level astral beings, gives much the same feeling as an orgasm during physical sex, only magnified about a thousand times. It is not something to play with, but should be used for definite, constructive purposes. It is love in the purest form, which seeks only to do good, and to create positive changes; love which gives without taking; love which is the basis of the power used by the Supreme Creative Force.

Eight

∞

Sublime Bliss

The ultimate astral relationship is with a high-level astral being or deity. This will not be something you yourself can force, accidentally wander into, or even initiate. The overture for such a relationship will only and always come from the higher being, and it will not be offered until you are considered ready for such an experience. It does not necessarily mean the melding of chakras, but can be simply a close friendship (a poor word to describe communion with such a being).

A relationship with a high-level being or deity is a sublime bliss which can't be imagined or described. The closest descriptions—and they fall far short of actuality—are the records left by Eastern yogis and Christian mystics. All these writers fumble for words, usually ending up drifting into the abstract. Yet, it is such an overwhelming event that those who experience it never forget it.

Although a relationship with a higher being can be desired simply for itself, there are certain side-benefits which come without seeking. The most prominent of these is the

143

acceleration of spiritual growth within the human who makes such a contact. It is what we might call divine love, an emotion which shoots off the scale of measurables. You will find many of your questions about spirituality instantly answered, and some of your personal views on the subject changed forever. You may even find all your ideas turned upside-down and completely reformed. Since each person is intensely individual, so will be the results of each experience.

This type of an astral relationship also makes it possible for you to establish a connection, or a firmer one, with the Goddess/God. Often your view of life, and what you are doing in it, becomes much clearer. Your psychic pipeline becomes unclogged, so to speak, making it easier to receive messages of guidance from your teachers and guides. You will *know* you are protected in the physical, something you may have been hesitant about at times. You may find yourself discarding your cherished goals and setting all new ones. On rare occasions, a person will have a total personality change.

Another benefit of this close communion with a higher being will be the growth and expansion of what we humans call "psychic talents." Healing and prophesying appear to be the talents most affected. People who have never shown the slightest interest in healing, for example, have suddenly found themselves bursting with healing energy. They find themselves healing incurable diseases merely by the touch of a hand. This can be a two-edged sword, for if you begin to revel in the power this healing gives you, or get caught up in the money you can make, the talent can disappear just as quickly as it came. Reporters and nay-sayers will follow you around, trying to prove you are a phony, completely disregarding what they see in the results.

Prophesying has always been both sought and feared by humans. Most humans have a love-hate attitude toward prophecy, wanting, yet not really wanting to know the future. "A prophet is never honored in his own country" is certainly true. People who have known you for years will not believe that you suddenly can see and know things which will happen in the future. Other people, who do accept you, can, or most often do, believe that you should be available at all hours of the day or night. Your personal life can become a shambles.

How, then, do you balance these blooming psychic talents with the negative atmosphere in which you live? You become very discrete in talking about or using them. When you do feel that you should use your talents, you do it in a low-key way, and never expect thanks. You do what you have to do, then walk away. The expansion of your psychic talents is a natural outcome of your spiritual growth—a sign that you are expanding and becoming more than you were.

Psychic Development Through Astral Travel

Intensification of psychic abilities appears to be a natural outcome of astral travel; but the greatest and strongest intensification of these talents comes after the establishment of a relationship with a higher-level being. Cornelius Agrippa wrote in *Occult Philosophy* that the human can gain prophetic powers through astral travel. In many cultures, the ability to astral travel is considered a prerequisite to developing such psychic talents as prophecy, healing, and performing magick. Psychic states of altered consciousness produce heightened awareness of all the senses, physical and non-physical. Going into an altered state of consciousness (astral traveling) will help you with the development of all forms of psychic talents or abilities. Astral travel appears to sensitize the traveler to the flows of astral energy and what is being created, and has been created in them. This occurs even if the traveler did not set out with this goal in mind.

Ancient cultures have always associated the development of psychic talents with the third eye in the center of the forehead. This is the sixth light center (the brow chakra), connected with the pineal gland, which lies approximately in the center of the brain. In some creatures, such as a certain New Zealand lizard, this gland appears to be a vestigial eye. The pineal gland secretes the chemical serotonin, one of the natural chemicals which produce a "high." The secretion of serotonin is greater during meditation, astral travel, and altered states of consciousness than at any other time. You might even call serotonin a "psychic hormone."

Psychic abilities which can be enhanced and more fully developed through travel on the astral planes are intuition, clairvoyance, psychometry, dowsing, clairaudience, precognition, telepathy, prediction, and telekinesis.

Intuition

Intuition appears to be emotionally based and connected with the solar plexus. Sometimes it is called a "gut feeling." It is the instant knowing that something should or should not be done, will or will not happen. Often, a person will say "I feel something is going to happen." They are responding to intuitive energy coming through their solar plexus light center. Intuition is probably the most commonly used of psychic talents, even by those who declare they have no such talent at all.

Clairvoyance

Defined as "clear seeing," The Celts of Ireland, Wales, and Scotland call this the "Second Sight." People with this ability can see spirits and entities in the astral world. It also enables the astral traveler to see clearly while out on the astral planes. Most of the time clairvoyance operates as seeing within the mind's eye, but sometimes it opens up to an actual physical seeing. For most people, this physical seeing occurs as flashes of movement or things seen in the peripheral vision. If one turns to look straight at the movement, there is nothing. When this ability is first actively cultivated, a person sees clouds of color and a continuous stream of images when they close their eyes to meditate.

Psychometry

One of the easiest of psychic talents to learn, psychometry is the ability to read the history of an object by touching it. William Denton, a professor of geology at Boston, came to the conclusion that everything in Nature can be imprinted in some way with its history through electrical impulses, and that this imprinted history can be detected and interpreted by the right brain. Psychometry is used to read the history, and sometimes the future, connected with objects such as jewelry, stones, or pottery. This information is in the form of vibrations caused by traumatic natural, or strong emotional events in the lives of people who handled or wore the objects. It is ordinarily not possible to get any information off objects made of plastic, leather, cloth, or paper. To read an imprint, the object is held between the palms of the hands, where there are secondary chakras. Then the person reading the object tells what symbols they see or emotional feelings they get.

Dowsing

A skill which is usually connected with the finding of water or minerals within the ground through the use of pendulums, willow wands, or bent metal coat hangers, a good dowser can also detect underground bunkers, tanks, and pipes. A pendulum can also be used as a divination tool. It isn't necessary to have a fancy crystal pendulum to perform this; something as simple as a ring tied to a piece of thread will work. You hold one end of the string between the thumb and forefinger of your power hand while your elbow is propped on a flat surface. (First you need to establish movements for yes, no, and undecided. For me, a yes answer is a forward and backward swing of the pendulum; no is a crosswise movement, while undecided is a circling.) Using a pendulum for divination will give you wrong answers unless you can avoid preconceptions while using it.

Clairaudience

The word means to "hear inwardly," and many religions call this the "voice of spirit." This can mean hearing a sudden disembodied voice with the physical ears, or hearing and understanding an astral voice with the inner ears. Usually, the first experience of clairaudience is being awakened by some non-present person calling your name. You may or may not recognize the voice. Sometimes the voice speaks a complete message. One woman awoke to "Don't drink coffee." It was such a firm statement that she hasn't touched coffee since. Another friend heard her father's voice saying "Come to me." She immediately packed and drove the hundred miles to find him in the hospital. Other messages never make any sense at all. Whatever you hear, please use common sense and don't rush off doing something drastic just because you heard a disembodied voice.

Precognition

Knowing something will happen before it does is a psychic skill which sometimes manifests through prophetic dreams, and at other times through flashes of just simple "knowing." Prophetic dreams can be very frustrating, as they seldom, if ever, give a time or date. About the only thing you can do is write them down and date them, then wait for the happening to occur. The most common prophetic dream is one of disaster. It is unusual for the disaster to affect you personally. For years, I have had prophetic dreams of mine accidents, airplane crashes, earthquakes, and volcanic eruptions. Sometimes the voice of an unseen being tells me where it will be, other times I deduce the area from the surroundings I see. Sometimes I am an uninvolved bystander, other times part of the action, although never afraid. I never get a date.

Telepathy

This is the ability to send a mental message from one person to another. When two people have strong connections, they can easily send and receive messages. Sometimes the sending appears to go in one direction, with one person sending and the other receiving. One couple I knew for years had a very strong telepathic link. The wife was an excellent sender, her husband only received, but he never missed a message or got it wrong.

Some animals become quite good at telepathy, too. The next time you find yourself the object of an intense stare from your pet, close your eyes and see what message or picture pops into your mind. If it is a picture of an empty food dish, try to change the picture to a full dish. Ten to one, you won't be able to make it stay full. When animals become adept at telepathy, they are extremely single-minded and focused.

Telekinesis

The ability to move objects without touching them—telekinesis—is a state of mind over matter. People with this ability can move pencils, influence compass needles and calculators, and cause floating corks to change direction. Technically, this ability could be used for the wrong purposes, such as those described in Raymond Buckland's novel, *The Committee.* *

Prediction

The use of crystals, tarot cards, or runes, is really a combination of several psychic abilities: psychometry, precognition, intuition, and clairvoyance. Scrying, or gazing into a crystal, pool of ink, cup of water, or something similar, is a very ancient art for reading both the future and the past. Reading tarot cards or runes is very similar to scrying. Almost anyone can memorize what cards or runes mean, but not everyone can put the finishing psychic touches on such a reading.

Because all astral entities communicate by telepathy, this is ordinarily the first talent to be strengthened through astral travel. Clairvoyance and clairaudience are greatly improved once you establish a strong telepathic communication link with an astral being, whether that being is one of your teachers or your astral lover. Because humans are usually so busy sending out emotional messages and signals from their solar plexus chakra—being so left-brain oriented—their intuition is down to a trickle, if that. Intuition begins to operate more freely when you start developing trust with your astral lover and teachers, when you allow your solar plexus to be open to their messages of love and their emotional signals.

Seeking a High-Level Lover

The astral entities who can help you to find this sublime bliss of a higher-level relationship are very high-level teachers, cer-

* *The Committee* by Raymond Buckland. St. Paul: Llewellyn, 1993.

tain deities, ancient priests and priestesses who trained years and lifetimes to reach their high level, and the Goddess/God. Not all teachers and guides will become astral lovers, so don't expect it. In fact, until you reach a certain level of spiritual development, it will be highly unlikely that any of your teachers will approach you for this type of relationship. After all, their primary purpose in being with you is as a teacher and spiritual confidante.

If one of your teachers should broach the idea of establishing a more intimate relationship with you, feel honored, but still consider carefully if this is something you want to do. It will be a higher energy form of chakra-melding, and will create strong changes in your life. Such a relationship with a high-level teacher will aid you in spiritual growth and create a very special connection between the two of you on all levels of being. If you don't feel at ease, confident, and ready for such an experience, tell them so. Any high-level teacher will understand, not push you, be willing to let you take however much time you need to decide, and never quibble about your decision.

In all forms of higher astral love, you will never begin a chakra-melding lower than the brow chakra in the center of your forehead. Next, the crown chakras will be connected. When this has been accomplished, the energy will rush downward, opening each chakra in turn. Often, a high-level being will only connect with your brow chakra the first few times. This appears necessary in order to acclimate your astral and physical bodies to the new and more powerful astral energy. While your brow chakras are connected, you may experience a rush of pictures running through your third eye. These pictures may be silent or accompanied by garbled sound, as if you were exposed to film running at top speed. For days after such an experience, you may find your forehead feeling slightly uncomfortable. It will feel as if the muscles are quickly expanding and contracting as in a spasm. This is a natural physical sensation; the third eye in your astral body is being exercised. What you experience in one body is felt in another.

When your high-level astral lover connects with both your brow and crown chakras, you will probably come back from the experience with a sense of unearthly euphoria. Your dreams may become suddenly symbolic in nature, be in vivid colors, and you will remember more of them. You may become so astrally active and involved in nightly dreaming of such intensity, that you feel exhausted during the day. If this happens, call upon your teachers and explain the situation. Ask them to cut down the intensity of your dreams so you can get some rest. Since astral beings are not hampered by a physical body and its needs, they often forget to take that into consideration when working with astral-traveling humans.

When you and your high-level astral lover get to the full chakra-melding—from the brow to the crown and then straight down through them all to the root center—you will find the experience spiritually intense. After you return to your physical body, however, you may experience some rather upsetting physical symptoms for a time. Since this full procedure aligns and cleanses your chakras from top to bottom, this should not be a surprise. You may find yourself extremely sensitive to loud noises, the vibrations of other people (particularly the negative kind), nervous for no apparent reason, nauseated by certain odors, even going through periods of laughing and crying over the smallest things. You won't necessarily be on a roller coaster of emotions or great highs or deep lows, just "drunk" on life itself. You need to pamper yourself until you adjust to the new, and to you unusual openness of your chakras.

What this high-level chakra-melding does is release the Kundalini energy under controlled guidance of an advanced being. Christian mystics called this state of being "ecstasy," while the Hindu mystics refer to it as "drunk on the divine." If the release of the Kundalini under these conditions produces such a reaction, you can image what would happen if it were deliberately raised by a person not knowledgeable and without any control. Such interaction with a high-level astral being is one of the most spiritual expressions of pure love that there is. Chakra-melding with your usual astral lover will make you feel loved and no longer lonely, but such connection with a high-level being will fill you with such sublime bliss that you *know* you are loved and watched over by the Goddess/God. You will never again feel totally abandoned to wander guideless through life. You will seek this spiritual experience again and again, because it is so beautiful, so comforting, such indescribable bliss.

The sublime bliss from an astral relationship, particularly one with a higher being, can help you in more ways than being no longer lonely. These high-level beings are the ones who can work the strongest of astral magick with you. They are knowledgeable experts on how to gather and fashion astral energy into manifested form, and how to see into the future to be sure that what you want will not hinder you later. They also will keep you wanting to meet them until they decide your development is at the correct stage. You must seek them sincerely and often in meditation and ritual, waiting patiently until they make their appearance. You work on their timetable, not they on yours.

The following meditation will help you seek such a high-level astral lover. Even though you may not experience immediate results, the meditation itself will help you in balancing yourself, as well as prepare for such a meeting in the future.

Meditation to Attract a High-Level Lover

Prepare for your meditation as usual. Visualize yourself surrounded by the white light for protection. Relax your body from your feet up to your head. Make a stop at the well and dump all the negatives in your life. Go to your astral temple or sacred place. Sit in your chair before the altar and think of why you want to attract a high-level lover. Be very truthful with your answers. If you lie, even to yourself, you will jeopardize all you have worked for.

As you sit before the altar, you hear the faint sounds of etheric music, the most beautiful you have ever heard, coming from all around you, though you don't see anyone. You feel this music subtly changing and raising your vibrations, until you feel as if you are going to float away. A brilliant white light forms high over the altar. It begins to pulsate with all the colors of the rainbow, like a prism swinging in a beam of sunlight. Slowly, this light lengthens and shapes itself into a human form. It descends until the being within it stands before the altar. The bright light fades away until only the being's robe is glowing with power.

You feel a jolt of excitement as you rise to greet this high-level being. She or he reaches out to take your hands. You feel as if you could explode with joy and happiness as this being smiles at you. She or he gives you a name by which she or he will be known to you. The two of you talk about your spiritual development, and what is needed in your physical life to help you gain this development. The high-level being asks if you are certain you want to meld chakras at this time. Whatever your answer, this being will respect your wishes.

If you desire to meld chakras, the two of you stand face to face before the altar. The white light descends to cover you. You feel a gentle beam of energy going to your brow chakra. Your third eye begins to rapidly pulse in response. Another beam opens your crown chakra, and you feel a desire for spiritual growth like a longing. One by one, the lower chakras begin to open, from the top down, flushing out blockages and purifying your entire astral form. When the root chakra is reached, you feel a sudden surge of Kundalini energy rising to spray like a fountain through your crown chakra.

Your body quivers in response to all this energy. The high-level being moves closer until both your bodies are first touching, then interpenetrating each other. The fountaining energy from both your crown chakras swirls around your forms like a whirlpool. The ecstasy is beyond anything you have ever experienced. Slowly, the high-level being moves back from you and lowers the energy flow. As you stand gazing into her or his beautiful eyes, you begin to realize the reasons for striving for higher spiritual attainment. The astral being steps down the energy still further until you are once again within your own vibrations. The high-level entity kisses you gently, then disappears.

You may wish to stay a while longer in your astral sacred place before returning to the Earth plane. When you want to return, think of your physical body and slide into it.

Once you have undergone an experience such as this, there will always be a part of you which will strive to return to that high level of vibration. This is because you have tasted the power from which you evolved, and you want to go "home." However, you are in a physical body to learn lessons and perfect your spiritual growth, so don't allow yourself to avoid your present responsibilities by returning to such a union too often. You can lose perspective and common sense

needed to function in everyday life. Your new high-level lover
will help to keep you in reality mode by lecturing you, or by
simply not appearing if you overdo.

If you are a practitioner of magick, you can use both the
attracting meditation and the following ritual to prepare the
way for a high-level astral being to meet with you. Your present magickal tradition doesn't matter, unless you are a
Satanist or into black magick in any form. (In that case, it is
highly unlikely you would be reading this book.) Practitioners
of magick on a regular basis understand quite well that it is
necessary to repeat certain rituals, and how some magickal
procedures need to build one upon another until the power is
great enough for results to be seen. Patience, concentration,
and determination are the key words in many types of magick.

Ritual to Attract a High-Level Being

This is best done during a waxing or Full Moon for the most
powerful positive benefits. You will need frankincense
incense, a white candle, a little salt, a chalice of water, and a
wand. If you plan to do the Attracting Meditation during the
central part of this ritual, place a chair before the altar on
which to sit.

Set up your altar with the white candle in the center and
to the back. Light the incense. With your wand in your power
hand, walk a clockwise circle about your ritual area. Point the
wand at the floor and say:

> *This circle is sealed with the highest of powers.*
> *Here I create a doorway between the worlds, a*
> *place where a high-level being may come and be*
> *with me.*

Return to the altar. Hold your hand, palm down over the water. Say:

> *This water of life is purified and blessed. May it*
> *wash away all impurities.*

Hold your palm over the salt and say:

> *This salt of earthly energies is purified and*
> *blessed. May it cast out all harmful vibrations.*

Put a pinch of salt into the water. Carry the chalice around the edges of your ritual circle, lightly sprinkling the water as you go. Return to the altar and set aside the water chalice. Light the white candle while mentally calling to a high-level astral being. Stand with your arms upraised and say:

> *I appeal to the highest astral planes for a com-*
> *panion. May one come to me here in this sacred*
> *place, a companion who will help me with my*
> *spiritual growth and seeking. I ask that you*
> *make yourself known to me in some way so that*
> *I may feel your presence.*

Now watch for changes in the candle flame, and be sensitive to changes in the vibrations of the room. If you see or feel anything usual, say:

> *Greetings and welcome!*

Now is the time to talk directly to this high-level entity as if he or she stood physically before you. Talk about what you would like to accomplish with your spiritual seeking, and ask for suggestions that would help you in your endeavors. Listen carefully!

If you plan to do the Attracting Meditation, sit in your chair and go off to your astral sacred temple. The high-level being may make an appearance at your altar there. When you are ready to close your ritual circle, return to the altar, raise your arms, and say:

> *My thanks to all who have helped me here. Go in*
> *peace and love, and blessings be upon you. This*
> *ritual is ended.*

Take your wand in your power hand and make a backward sweep across the edge of your cast circle. You may leave the white candle to burn out in a safe place, or you may extinguish it and save it for another time.

The ultimate high-level astral relationship is with the Goddess or the God. (The Pagan God has absolutely no similarities to the Christian deity.) At some time you will want to establish a loving relationship with both the Goddess and the God, so don't let your present physical sex or sexual preference stand in the way. How far this relationship will go will be determined by your state of spiritual growth, not your desires for such a union. The following meditation will help you to make contact, but is no assurance that you will undergo any melding.

Meeting with the Goddess and the God

Prepare for your meditation as usual. Surround yourself with white light. Relax your body from the feet up to the head. Stop by the well and dump your negatives. This is especially important for this meeting, because old hatreds and fears will keep you from making full contact.

You find yourself alone in a grassy meadow. Before you stretches a deep, ancient forest. The tall trees stand in mystic ranks across one side of the meadow, then climb the lower heights of steep mountain peaks. The forest stops among the rocky cliffs, leaving the towering peaks to hide alone among the heavy clouds.

You walk along the edge of the thick forest until you discover an almost hidden path which twists and turns among the trees. As you follow the path, you notice alternate patches of sunlight and shadow which fall upon the trail. The soft notes of panpipes sound in the distance, and birds answer among the tall trees. Neither the birds nor the forest animals are afraid or threaten you. The deeper you follow the path into the forest, the closer you come to the sound of the panpipes.

The path twists around a huge, bare rock with sunlight through the thick fir branches creating moving patterns upon it. The panpipes sound above you. You look up and see Pan himself sitting there, pipes in hand. He bounds down from the rock and stands beside you, smiling. He has been waiting to accompany you into the forest. Pan's greeting is friendly as he walks along beside you.

Soon the forest opens upon a large, circular, grassy area. In the center is a rustic stone altar decorated with beautiful wildflowers. At one end of the altar stands a golden incense burner; at the other end is a silver burner. Elves, gnomes, faeries, wood sprites, and other elementals stand around the clearing and the two rocky thrones behind the altar. On these two thrones sit two powerful beings: the Goddess and the God.

As Pan leads you to the thrones, you can feel strength radiating from these two Otherworld entities. The power is so strong and so all-encompassing that you are a little afraid as you stand there looking up into their eyes. The Goddess holds out Her hands to you. You walk forward until your hands lie within Hers. Her beautiful eyes penetrate into your deepest secret being; all is known to Her. She draws you forward onto Her lap. Like the Great Mother She is, the Goddess holds you as if you were a child; Her loving thoughts sweep away all loneliness and fear. With great gentleness, you feel your upper chakras, then your heart chakra melding with Hers. The power is carefully controlled, for you could not exist if you melded fully with the Goddess.

You feel as if everything about you, except your spirit, is melting away into nothingness. You may be given advice which will help you on your spiritual path. Then the power is slowly withdrawn. The Goddess smiles and directs you to the God, who waits beside Her. As you stand before Him, you are overwhelmed by the God's penetrating gaze. As with the Goddess, He sees everything about you and still offers His love. You step closer, and He gathers you into His strong arms. You feel your upper chakras, then your heart chakra begin to meld with His. The power is just as gentle and controlled as with the Goddess, but is of a totally different kind. You feel yourself sinking deep into His energy as you would sink into a quiet pond. Your body quivers as it is cleansed and rebalanced. He may give you messages to help you in your life.

As the God gently disconnects the power flow, you take a deep breath. You rise to stand once more before the thrones, looking up at these powerful deities. At this time, the Goddess and God may talk to you about personal decisions and events with which you are dealing in your everyday life. They may give you an astral symbol or gift, which will probably appear later in the physical realm. At last, Pan takes your hand and leads you back through the forest. At the edge of the meadow, he winks and smiles. You think of your physical body and return to it.

This meeting with the Goddess and the God will probably change as you grow spiritually. No two such meditations will ever be the same. If you are depressed or overwhelmed by sadness or a personal tragedy, meeting with the Goddess and the God is the most comforting thing you can do. The results from such a meeting will be subtle at first, but each time you seek out these deities, the power flow will increase until you experience an almost sexual flow between you. The power flow from the Goddess and the God is of a much higher nature than that from your astral lover or even a high-level astral being. It will not be sexually gratifying, but soul gratifying.

Nine

❧

Astral Sex Magick

Almost all people who desire to learn about magick, or who have taken the plunge and work with it, have experienced magickal endeavors in past lives. Some practiced magick more than others. You would not be interested in magick today if you hadn't had a taste of it in another lifetime. Delving into your Akashic records in the astral is the only way to find out about past lives connected in some way with magick.

Beware of anyone telling you not to use magick to help yourself to a better life. That is simply a trap to keep you under control; using magick is one of the big "thou shalt nots" of orthodox religions. Of course, using magick to better yourself should never be at the expense of other people. Knowing how to use magick means you can become an independent person, no longer relying on others to make your decisions in everyday or spiritual life. Magick leads to greater spirituality; the very roots of all positive magick lie in a belief in a Supreme Creator and a spiritual afterlife.

The ancient Egyptians taught that the mind had the power to set vibrations into motion, and that these vibrations would eventually manifest in physical form. They also said that humans were made up of the same elemental forces which were used to build the universe. They called these forces the seven astral rays, perhaps another description of the seven light centers of the astral body.

Since only ten percent of your potential and power are available to you in your regular state of consciousness, you need to go into the astral planes to tap the remaining ninety percent. If you limit yourself to *physically* working magick, you are avoiding the use of the most powerful part of your consciousness.

There are definite differences between physical and astral magick. Physical magick requires actual physical and mental work. The results must pass from the physical realm into the astral realm to be built of cosmic energy, before it can return to the physical as a desired result. Astral magick is much more difficult and demanding, but can also be more effective and show results more quickly. The magician has to know how to get onto the astral planes, and then use complete visualization right down to and including the senses. You have to learn how to handle and control astral energies and shape them into the form you desire, so they can manifest in the physical. You have to be very specific in astral magick, otherwise, you will get mixed results in the manifestation.

The astral planes are a source of unlimited potential power for working magick, creating manifestations to appear later in your life, or healing yourself and others. You merely have to learn how to weave that power into creative strands of energy, which you then can use to create a thoughtform powered with the intent which you give it. The very air we breathe is full of astral energy. It is this energy which flows into all of our light centers, opens the third eye, and creates or manifests our intense desires or fears. Energy from the astral planes can be deliberately molded and reshaped into any form you wish. Astral energy is unlimited, has no preconceived positive or negative powers, and is available to anyone.

To start the flow of astral energy, begin by having a very clear mental picture of the result you want. You must intensely want to gain this result; if it is only a half-hearted desire, it will not be strong enough to materialize. These desires are thoughtforms before they manifest into actuality. They have a definite shape and color, and can be seen by psychics. A weak thoughtform will disintegrate before it manifests. A clear, strong thought may take time to manifest, but it will reproduce itself in the physical world.

When working magick for a desired end, be certain you have considered all the possible results. Think over the smallest of details, seeing how everything might react in some other part of your plan. If you overlook any aspect, it might pop up later and derail the whole thing.

We have more control over, and more possibility of changing, individual future karma than we have of affecting group karma, or even that of a nation or the world as a whole. This is because fewer people are involved in individual karma than national or world karma. The more people involved in a particular future event, the more likely it is to change suddenly. If you see a national or even regional event where the vast majority of people involved don't want change, you will not be likely to influence the situation.

Individual futures are in a more flexible state. Even in individual future events which seem already to be set, the magician can make small changes. Wisdom lies in learning where to put the pressure. A tiny bit of pressure applied to a specific part of an upcoming individual event may be enough to create a totally different outcome.

No matter what any psychic has told you, or what you believe will happen, if a situation is negative, try to make small changes in that future event. Never be a martyr to circumstances if you can help it, and you can always help it to some degree. Never accept that karma can't be changed, and be willing to make all the changes you can. Don't be jealous of the good fortune of another person, even if that person is one of your enemies. By raising your thoughts into a positive mode, you can charge your aura with their good luck, thus improving your own future.

The Magickal Child

Many times in books, and when talking with people in the magickal field, you come across the term "magickal child." Astral sex magick is much like physical sex magick, but on a higher level and much more powerful. The energy is allowed to build between two beings while they are concentrating on a desired manifestation. When a high point is reached, the power is released. The energy raised from sexual power created by chakra-melding can be put to any magickal use. It is the responsibility of the participants to have high objectives and not use it to harm anyone.

There are definite results of a union between a mortal and an astral being, whether or not the energy raised is directed into a magickal purpose. It is only common sense that you should direct this energy to a positive result, rather than let it fly around the astral planes, becoming something on its own. Astral intercourse through chakra-melding creates what is called a "magickal child." This is what is meant by the legends of children born of such unions between a mortal and an astral being. A mortal woman may desire a child, but be unsuccessful in her efforts to get pregnant. If she is knowledgeable about astral sex magick, she can unite with an astral being, turn the raised power inward, and create a physical pregnancy. Merlin and other such legendary "children of gods" were conceived in this way. Of course, such a woman should desire the highest spiritual child possible, so she should be very careful in her choice of astral partners. All the mental, emotional, and spiritual characteristics of both partners will be inherent in the baby.

Another form of "magickal child" is the "mental child," the desired physical outcome of an event or fulfillment of a wish. Any time one does magick with a definite result in mind, one is attempting to create a mental child. For example, perhaps you need a new and better job. You keep this thought in mind while uniting with an astral being, then release the energy to form and be born in the physical world, resulting in a positive change in your job outlook.

The birth or creation of a "spiritual child" is the most complex, the most demanding, and the one for which there is no excuse if you make a mistake. The spiritual child only has existence on the astral planes. It is a highly advanced technique used to bring into existence an astral being of high spiritual values, who can have a positive impact on both levels of being: astral and physical. A few of these spiritual children are ultimately born into the physical as great teachers. The creation of such a child is a tremendous responsibility, for if you get it wrong, you will have loosed a being of great power, who may harm rather than help. If you create anything less than a high spiritual being, you will pay for the mistake for many lifetimes. There is absolutely no reprieve.

There are other benefits to astral sex magick other than creating a magickal child to manifest as a physical or spiritual child. Most such magick will be used to benefit your everyday life directly. By carefully choosing the high-level lover who works with you, you will eventually form a rapport with your high-level companion, which will improve your physical magick and help you in your spiritual growth. Once established, such an intimate relationship will continue through several lifetimes, strengthening as it is used.

The very basis of sexual magick, whether physical or astral, is thought control during the crucial moments when the power peaks. Thought control is simply controlling sexual energy raised during intercourse. This is a great deal harder than it sounds. If you doubt this, try controlling what you are thinking the next time you make love with your mate and your emotions reach their high point in the act. In addition, both partners in the sexual union must agree on the desired outcome, and be proficient in control of the energy raised.

Lovemaking with magick in mind certainly isn't a desirable activity for every time you want to make love. After all, most lovemaking is for mutual expression of intense feelings and for physical gratification. Lovemaking for these reasons is a part of human life, built in from the very beginning of the human race.

Preventing Psychic Sabotage

The more advanced you become magickally and spiritually, on the physical plane or in the astral realms, the more likely you are to eventually run into someone (physical or astral) who wants you to fail. If they can't sabotage you directly by putting thoughts of "wrong, sinful, or evil" in your mind, they will attack you psychically or astrally. This becomes a potential danger if the being in question is knowledgeable about magick. However, you can still be in danger if the person doesn't know or believe in magick, and only projects constant hateful, negative thoughts in your direction. Most magicians and astral travelers aren't in much danger from their fellow humans; the greatest dangers come from negative astral entities who resent your progress in astral magick. They will attempt to disrupt your astral magickal rituals whenever they can. One way to keep them from interfering is to always circle yourself and your astral lover with a glowing circle of white light before you begin the chakra-melding. No astral entity or astral traveler can cross this circle of white light unless you invite them in. It also helps to be very specific about your lover's vibrations when you send out the mental call to meet you on the astral planes.

On rare occasions you might incur the interest of some powerful, discarnate, negative magician. If one of these should approach you in the astral, you won't have to guess who or what you see; you will instantly know by the slimy feel of his or her vibrations. If this should happen, stay close to your astral lover, who will know what to do and whom to call upon for help. Whatever happens, if you and your lover should get separated, return at once to your physical body.

Problems can also arise from deceased humans who were believers in orthodox religions in their earthly life or lives, and who firmly believe that astral magick, or any magick for that matter, is evil. However much they would like to believe to the contrary, the power of these types of entities is not very strong. It is easier to deflect the ill-will of these discarnate humans than it is to deal with powerful, negative astral entities. Call on the astral police, and have them removed from your presence. There is no way they can resist the order to go elsewhere.

The most disruptive influence the vast majority of astral travelers encounter are not discarnate beings or negative astral entities, but created negative thoughtforms. These thoughtforms can have been created by anyone thinking strong, negative emotional thoughts about you—including yourself. When one of these thoughtforms attempts to interfere with your astral magick, both you and your astral lover should send beams of cosmic energy through your brow chakras against the thoughtform. This will either change its polarity from negative to positive, or reduce it to its original neutral particles of energy. You really want to change its polarity, because breaking it out of its pattern will return its primary energy to the sender. If the creator was you, even though you built it subconsciously, you don't want all that negative energy zeroing in on you.

Whether you are out on the astral or in your physical body when you are attacked by astral entities, your first line of defense should be to shout for the astral police to protect you. Your teachers and astral lovers will also defend you with all the means at their disposal. If this doesn't stop the problem, you need to fill your whole immediate area with white light. Wearing a consecrated amulet on your physical body while astral traveling is another method of repelling most astral annoyances. This can be any stone or symbol which has a deep spiritual meaning for you. To consecrate it, pass the amulet through the smoke of frankincense incense. The vast majority of astral attacks are not very strong and can be deflected, or their polarity changed, with determination and help from your astral lover. Never consider yourself defenseless while out on the astral planes.

Because astral sex magick takes patience to learn to do properly, and this means pleasant practice with your astral lover, most thoughtforms or entities will try to irritate and interrupt you so you will give up and quit trying. If you refuse to stop practicing this type of magick, eventually the thoughtforms and entities will give up and go away.

With all one can accomplish through the practice of astral sex magick, you really don't want to quit before you see the fantastic results you can produce. Through astral magick you can create healings for specific people, or add to what is being done by other astral groups for peace in the world. You will also experience many side benefits in your life. Your health, prosperity, happiness, and spiritual growth will move into positive levels. Your personal relationships with astral beings, as friends and lovers, will dispel your loneliness and help you keep a better mental attitude. You may even find yourself setting up a totally new set of goals in areas of interest you had never before considered. The possibilities are endless.

The best and highest rewards you get from astral loving will not be the mental and emotional satisfaction, but the strong spiritual ties you develop. Even though you might not start out with this in mind, it will happen. Your relationship with the Goddess/God will be stronger than it has ever been. You will have touched the source of unconditional love and power with a fingertip, and will always be yearning to explore it in greater depth. That is the great secret behind the meaning of astral love and sex magick.

Bibliography

Astral Love and Magick

Blamires, Steve. *The Irish Celtic Magical Tradition*. UK: Harper/Thorsons, 1992.

Brennan, J. H. *Astral Doorways*. UK: Aquarian Press, 1971.

Buckland, Raymond. *The Committee*. St. Paul: Llewellyn Publications, 1993.

Cavendish, Richard. *The Black Arts*. New York: G.P. Putnam's Sons, 1967. (Not a book of black magick.)

Conway, D. J. *By Oak, Ash & Thorn: Modern Celtic Shamanism*. St. Paul: Llewellyn Publications, 1995.

———. *Flying Without a Broom*. St. Paul: Llewellyn Publications, 1995.

Curtin, Jeremiah. *Myths and Folk Tales of Ireland*. New York: Dover, 1975. Originally published 1890.

DeGivry, Grillot. *Witchcraft, Magic & Alchemy*. New York: Dover, 1971.

Denning, Melita and Osborne Phillips. *Astral Projection: the Out-of-Body Experience*. St. Paul: Llewellyn Publications, 1991.

Duffy, Maureen. *The Erotic World of Faery*. Harrisburg: Stackpole Books, 1971.

Eliade, Mircea. *Shamanism: Archaic Techniques of Ecstasy*. Princeton, NJ: Princeton University Press, 1964.

Evans-Wentz, W. Y. *The Fairy Faith in Celtic Countries*. New York: Citadel Press, 1990.

Fox, Oliver. *Astral Projection*. New Hyde Park: University Books, 1962.

Gantz, Jeffrey. *Early Irish Myths & Sagas*. UK: Penguin Books, 1981.

Graves, Robert. *The White Goddess*. New York: Farrar, Straus & Giroux, 1966.

Guiley, Rosemary Ellen. *The Encyclopedia of Ghosts and Spirits*. New York: Facts on File Books, 1992.

Hazlitt, W. Carew. *Faiths and Folklore of the British Isles*. 2 vols. New York: Benjamin Blom, 1965.

Jackson, A. *The Symbol Stories of Scotland*. Stromness: The Orkney Press, 1984.

Judith, Anodea. *Wheels of Life: A User's Guide to the Chakra System*. St. Paul: Llewellyn Publications, 1993.

Jung, Carl G. *The Archetypes and the Collective Unconscious*. Princeton: Princeton University Press, 1990.

Mookerjee, Ajit. *Kundalini: The Arousal of the Inner Energy*. New York: Destiny Books, 1983.

Muldoon, Sylvan and Hereward Carrington. *The Projection of the Astral Body*. York Beach: Samuel Weiser, 1989. Originally published 1929.

Paracelsus. Guterman, N. trans. *Selected Writings*. UK: Routledge & Kegan Paul, 1951.

Shaw, Indris. *The Sufis*. UK: Octagon Press, 1964.

Spann, David B. *The Otherworld in Early Irish Literature*. Ann Arbor: University of Michigan Press, 1969.

Stewart, J. R. *Robert Kirk: Walker Between Worlds: A New Edition of the Secret Commonwealth of Elves, Fauns and Fairies*. UK: Element Books, 1990. Written in 1690 or 1691.

Thompson, C. J. S. *The Mysteries and Secrets of Magic*. New York: Barnes & Noble, 1993.

Turville, Petrie E.O.G. *Myth and Religion of the North*. Westport: Greenwood Press, 1975.

Yeats, W. B. and Lady Isabella Augusta Gregory. *A Treasury of Irish Myth, Legend and Folklore.* New York: Avenel Books, 1986. Originally published in 1888.

Physical Sex Magick

Culling, Louis T. *Sex Magick.* St. Paul: Llewellyn Publications, 1986.

Douglas, Nik and Penny Slinger. *Sexual Secrets.* New York: Destiny Books, 1979.

Farrar, Janet and Stewart Farrar. *Eight Sabbats for Witches.* UK: Robert Hale, 1981.

———. *The Witches' Way.* UK: Robert Hale, 1984.

Fortune, Dion. *Moon Magic.* York Beach: Samuel Weiser, 1985.

———. *The Sea Priestess.* York Beach: Samuel Weiser, 1985.

Kraig, Donald Michael. *Modern Magick: Eleven Lessons in the High Magickal Arts.* St. Paul: Llewellyn Publications, 1989.

Mumford, Jonn. *Ecstasy Through Tantra.* St. Paul: Llewellyn Publications, 1988.

Index

Healing, 15, 23, 25, 28-29, 32,
    42, 52, 96, 110-112, 123-
    124, 129-130, 144-145,
    164
Higher astral love, 151

incubus, 19, 136
intuition, 18, 56, 104-105,
    111-112, 146, 150

Karma, 4, 21, 54, 89-91, 93,
    165-166

Lady Wilde, 77
left brain, 62
low-level entities, 19, 24, 43,
    55, 61, 92, 126, 134

Magickal child, 38, 166-167
Melatonin, 9
Mental child, 167
Merlin, 39, 94, 167
Mexico, 32, 39

nature spirits, 4, 55, 76, 79, 94

Paracelsus, 9-10
pendulum, 116, 148
plane of darkness, 54
precognition, 146, 148, 150
prophesying, 144
psychic abilities, 114, 145-146,
    150
psychic lice, 17, 58, 70
Psychometry, 146-147, 150

right brain, 7, 147
Ring of fire, 61
Robert Kirk, 38, 77-78

Serotonin, 9, 146
Seven levels, 3, 53-54, 96

Shaman, 2, 39, 78, 97
Silver cord, 6-7
Spiritual body, 6, 63
Spiritual child, 167
stones, 30-32, 104, 147
subconscious mind, 7-8, 11, 17,
    60, 64, 102
succubus, 19, 136

Teacher-guides, 50, 54, 65, 68,
    88, 125-126
telekinesis, 146, 149
telepathy, 14, 64, 146, 149-150
Terror of the Threshold, 67
Theta, 8
Thomas the Rhymer, 77
thoughtforms, 4, 55, 57-60,
    65-66, 69-70, 165, 169-
    170

Yeats (W. B.), 77

On the following pages you will find listed, with their current prices, some of the books now available on related subjects. Your book dealer stocks most of these and will stock new titles in the Llewellyn series as they become available. We urge your patronage.

To Order Books and Tapes

If your book store does not carry the titles described on the following pages, you may order them directly from Llewellyn by sending the full price in U.S. funds, plus postage and handling (see below).

Credit Card Orders: VISA, MasterCard, American Express are accepted. Call us toll-free within the United States and Canada at 1-800-THE-MOON.

Special Group Discount: Because there is a great deal of interest in group discussion and study of the subject matter of this book, we offer a 20% quantity discount to group leaders or agents. Our Special Quantity Price for a minimum order of five copies of *Astral Love* is $51.80 cash-with-order. Include postage and handling charges noted below.

Postage and Handling: Include $4 postage and handling for orders $15 and under; $5 for orders over $15. There are no postage and handling charges for orders over $100. Postage and handling rates are subject to change. We ship UPS whenever possible within the continental United States; delivery is guaranteed. Please provide your street address as UPS does not deliver to P.O. boxes. Orders shipped to Alaska, Hawaii, Canada, Mexico and Puerto Rico will be sent via first class mail. Allow 4-6 weeks for delivery.

International Orders: Airmail—add retail price of each book and $5 for each non-book item (audiotapes, etc.); Surface mail—add $1 per item. Minnesota residents add 7% sales tax.

Mail orders to:

Llewellyn Worldwide
P.O. Box 64383-K161
St. Paul, MN 55164-0383, U.S.A.

For customer service, call (612) 291-1970.

Flying Without a Broom
Astral Projection and the Astral World
by D. J. Conway

Astral flight has been described through history as a vital part of spiritual development and a powerful aid to magickal workings. In this remarkable volume, respected author D.J. Conway shows how anyone can have the keys to a profound astral experience.

This how-to includes historical lore, astral plane basics, and a simplified learning process to get you "off the ground." You'll learn simple exercises to strengthen your astral abilities as well as a variety of astral techniques. After the basics, use the astral planes to work magick and healings; contact teachers, guides, or lovers; and visit past lives. You'll also learn how to protect yourself and others from the low-level entities encountered in the astral.

Through astral travel you will expand your spiritual growth, strengthen your spiritual efforts, and bring your daily life to a new level of integration and satisfaction.

1-56718-164-3, 224 pp., 6 x 9, softcover $13.00

Moon Magick
Myth & Magic, Crafts & Recipes, Rituals & Spells
by D. J. Conway

No creature on this planet is unaffected by the power of the Moon. Its effects range from making us feel energetic or adventurous to tense and despondent. By putting Moon energy to work for you, you can learn to plan projects, work and travel at the best times.

Moon Magick explains how each of the 13 lunar months is connected with a different type of energy and provides modern rituals and spells for tapping this energy and celebrating the Moon phases. Each chapter describes new Pagan rituals related to that particular Moon, plus lore, holidays, spells, meditations and suggestions for foods, drinks and decorations to accompany your rituals. This book includes two dictionaries of Moon deities and symbols. *Moon Magick* will show you how to let your life flow with the power and rhythms of the Moon to benefit your physical, emotional and spiritual well-being.

1-56718-167-8, 320 pp., 7 x 10, illus., softcover $14.95

The Dream Warrior
Book One of the Dream Warrior Trilogy
a Novel by D. J. Conway

Danger, intrigue, and adventure seem to follow dauntless Corri Farblood wherever she goes. Sold as a child to the grotesque and sinister master thief Grimmel, Corri was forced into thievery at a young age. In fact, at eighteen, she's the best thief in the city of Hadliden—but she also possesses an ability to travel the astral plane, called "dream-flying," that makes her even more unique. Her talents make her a valuable commodity to Grimmel, but Corri escapes with the aid of a traveling sorcerer, who has a quest of his own to pursue...

Journey across the wide land of Sar Akka with Corri, the sorcerer Imandoff Silverhair, and the warrior Takra Wind-Rider as they search for an ancient place of power. As Grimmel's assassins relentlessly pursue her, Corri battles against time and her enemies to solve the mystery of her heritage and to gain control over her potent clairvoyant gifts...to learn the meaning of companionship and love...and to finally confront a fate that will test her powers and courage to the limit.

1-56718-169-4, 360 pp., 5¼ x 8, softcover $14.95

The Llewellyn Practical Guide to Astral Projection
The Out-of-Body Experience
by Denning & Phillips

Yes, your consciousness can be sent forth, out of the body, with full awareness and return with full memory. You can travel through time and space, converse with nonphysical entities, obtain knowledge by nonmaterial means, and experience higher dimensions.

Guidance is also given to the Astral World itself: what to expect, what can be done—including the ecstatic experience of Astral Sex between two people who project together into this higher world where true union is consummated free of the barriers of physical bodies.

0-87542-181-4, 266 pp., 5¼ x 8, illus., softcover $8.95

Ecstasy Through Tantra

by Dr. Jonn Mumford

Dr. Jonn Mumford makes the occult dimension of the sexual dynamic accessible to everyone. One need not go up to the mountaintop to commune with Divinity: its temple is the body, its sacrament the communion between lovers. *Ecstasy Through Tantra* traces the ancient practices of sex magick through the Egyptian, Greek and Hebrew forms, where the sexual act is viewed as symbolic of the highest union, to the highest expression of Western sex magick.

Dr. Mumford guides the reader through mental and physical exercises aimed at developing psychosexual power; he details the various sexual practices and positions that facilitate "psychic short-circuiting" and the arousal of Kundalini, the Goddess of Life within the body. He shows the fundamental unity of Tantra with Western Wicca, and he plumbs the depths of Western sex magick, showing how its techniques culminate in spiritual illumination. Includes 14 full-color photographs.

0-87542-494-5, 190 pp., 6 x 9, color plates, softcover $12.95

Greenfire

Making Love with the Goddess
by Sirona Knight

Now you and your partner can apply the vast amounts of energy generated by sexual union and orgasm to improve every facet of your life, spirituality and relationship!

Greenfire offers an innovative approach to the goddess tradition in the area of sexual expression and exploration by joining elements of traditional Celtic Gwyddonic ritual and symbolism with tasteful erotic passages and guided fantasy. This book offers straightforward instruction for the solitary practitioner focusing on creating a viable relationship with one partner by merging with the divine aspects that exist inside each of us. *Greenfire* is your guide to attaining the oneness you've longed for between woman and man, goddess and god—and within yourself.

1–56718–386–7, 224 pp., 6 x 9, illus., softcover $14.95